T0305835

RESPONSIBLE INNOVATION
FROM CONCEPT TO PRACTICE

RESPONSIBLE
INNOVATION
FROM CONCEPT TO PRACTICE

Xavier Pavie
ESSEC Business School, France

Victor Scholten
University of Technology, The Netherlands

Daphné Carthy
ESSEC Business School, France

World Scientific

NEW JERSEY · LONDON · SINGAPORE · BEIJING · SHANGHAI · HONG KONG · TAIPEI · CHENNAI

Published by

World Scientific Publishing Co. Pte. Ltd.

5 Toh Tuck Link, Singapore 596224

USA office: 27 Warren Street, Suite 401-402, Hackensack, NJ 07601

UK office: 57 Shelton Street, Covent Garden, London WC2H 9HE

Library of Congress Cataloging-in-Publication Data
Pavie, Xavier, 1973–
    Responsible innovation : from concept to practice / by Xavier Pavie (ESSEC Business School,
France), Victor Scholten (University of Technology, The Netherlands) & Daphné Carthy (ESSEC
Business School, France).
        pages cm
    Includes bibliographical references and index.
    ISBN 978-9814525077
    1. Technological innovations--Management. 2. Diffusion of innovations--Management.
3. Organizational effectiveness. I. Title.
    HD45.P3925 2014
    658.4'063--dc23
                                                         2013027367

British Library Cataloguing-in-Publication Data
A catalogue record for this book is available from the British Library.

In-house Editors: Sandhya Venkatesh/Dipasri Sardar

Typeset by Stallion Press
Email: enquiries@stallionpress.com

Printed in Singapore

CONTENTS

ABOUT THE AUTHORS

Xavier Pavie

Xavier Pavie holds Master's Degrees in Management and Philosophy and a Ph.D. in the latter. Xavier has successfully held executive positions in leading companies for 15 years and in 2008 he was appointed Director of the Institute for Strategic Innovation & Services (ISIS) at ESSEC Business School. He is also research associate at IREPH (Institut Recherche Philosophique) — Université Paris Ouest.

Xavier's publications focus on philosophical approaches to innovation management and more particularly on the notion of performance. He has published several articles and a dozen of books on philosophy and on innovation.

Victor Scholten

Victor Scholten holds a Ph.D. in Entrepreneurship from Wageningen University. He is Assistant Professor in Technology-Based Entrepreneurship at Delft University of Technology, the Netherlands. Before joining Delft University of Technology in 2007, he held the position of Assistant Professor at Erasmus University in Rotterdam.

His current research interests are in academic spin-out companies, technology transfer to SMEs, responsible innovation and new business venturing, entrepreneurial teams and entrepreneurial networking strategies.

Daphné Carthy

Daphné Carthy holds a B.A. in International Business from Dublin City University and a Post-Graduate Diploma in International Business Development from Dublin Institute of Technology in Ireland. She is a Research Associate at the Institute for Strategic Innovation and Services (ISIS) at ESSEC Business School. Prior to joining ISIS, she worked as a market researcher and consultant in business development and marketing based in Paris and Düsseldorf.

Her current research areas of interest include the integration of responsibility into the innovation process as a strategy for achieving performance objectives.

ACKNOWLEDGMENTS

We wish to acknowledge the Institute for Strategic Innovation and Services (ISIS) of ESSEC Business School for helping us to develop the concept of responsible innovation over the past few years and particularly: Prof. Hervé Mathe, Luce Abrate, Simon Paranthoën and Viveka Gidwani.

We are very grateful to the many partners who contributed to enriching the debate on responsible innovation: members of the FAIR project and the Centre Francilien de l'Innovation, notably Michel Daigney, Gaëlle Hin, Doris Kirschner and Serge Gadbois.

Last but not least, we would like to express our gratitude to all students and speakers who took part in the responsible innovation course at ESSEC Business School over the last two years.

Xavier Pavie & Daphné Carthy

I appreciate the support and discussion I had with colleagues in the department of Values, Technology and Innovation of Delft University of Technology. The thinking and philosophical discussions with Prof. Jeroen van den Hoven and Prof. Ibo van de Poel helped me framing the concept of responsible innovation and translate it to practical value. Also the suggestions and reflections of Prof. Cees van Beers, Dap Hartmann and Patrick van der Duin contributed much to the further understanding of responsible innovation and the opportunities it provides for SMEs.

I also thank Frank O'Connor, Simon O'Rafferty and Merel Claes, when they were at the Ecodesign Centre in Wales, for their valuable leads which were central to the work that we conducted within the KARIM project and led to the inception of the present book.

Finally I wish to thank all the students that raised questions and helped us much in articulating our thoughts and make it understandable for a wider audience.

Victor Scholten

The research presented in this book was partly derived from actions undertaken as part of the KARIM (Knowledge Acceleration Responsible Innovation Metanetwork) project. Part of the INTERREG IVB North-West Europe strategic initiatives program, KARIM brings together eight partners from six States of North-West Europe (France, Germany, Great Britain, Ireland, the Netherlands and Switzerland). It aims to improve SME access to technology and innovation support services (in particular those related to responsible innovation projects), thereby boosting North-West Europe's competitiveness. The project's main objectives are to establish a definition of responsible innovation; to facilitate the transfer of knowledge across North-West Europe; to build a strategic network of innovation actors and to provide support for innovation.

INTRODUCTION

Understanding and Justifying the Need for Responsibility

On the 27th September 1962, amidst a context of rapid growth and development driven by a booming plastic industry and the expansion of large petrochemical companies, Rachel Carson published a groundbreaking work in the history of innovation: *"Silent Spring."* At the time, insect and bacterial infestations were causing vast destruction of crops across the United States, rendering a high proportion of agricultural produce unfit for consumption. Pesticides were eventually introduced as the ultimate solution for saving crops.[1]

A marine biologist and conservationist, Carson made a prediction that the birds pecking in the fields would die from ingesting the pesticides, leading to a silent spring season. Her theories and suggestion for an alternative solution to replace the constant use of pesticides which could prove to be extremely harmful to human health were seen as a nuisance and generated a storm of controversy. Fifty years later, websites still exist maintaining that Carson was wrong.[2]

In this modern day and age her alarm call is as topical as ever. A website of the American right-wing ultraliberal party advocates the free market, the *laisser-faire* policy, the freedom to use pesticides and set up environmental protection systems — all issues which reflect initial interrogations presented by Carson and Ayn Rand.[3] At this stage, a sense of unease prevails: How could we ignore the deaths of birds, or even human beings, which will have ingested the pesticides? The question of responsibility at the heart of innovation is now raised. We must innovate, that is a fact, but at what price?

---

[1]Carson, R (1962). *Silent Spring.* Boston: Houghton Mifflin Harcourt.
[2]http://rachelwaswrong.org/.
[3]Rand, A (1957). *Atlas Shrugged.* New York: Signet.

When innovation questions our humanity

There are numerous actors which claim to engage in responsible innovation: Sodexo, Unilever, L'Oréal, etc. Has the term become the new portmanteau word? What is responsible innovation?

In 2009, the first *"savior sibling"* was born in France. His parents already had a daughter who suffered from a genetic disease and whose cure depended on collecting stem cells from a sibling. The couple therefore, decided to have a second child for this purpose. In this case, instead of asking "should we do this or not?" The question should rather focus on "why and how should we do this?" The decision to conceive a *"savior sibling"* was discussed in privacy by the couple and with the doctors. Who has the right for such a solution and who hasn't? Is it a question of financial wealth or health system efficiency — in other words, is it solely intended for inhabitants of the northern hemisphere? Is it our wish to select individuals in this way? Does it make sense to give birth to a child in order to save another?

Making, cloning or improving life: this fundamental question is not recent. Humanity's need for progress can be found already in the Greek and Mayan mythologies. Prometheus is the benefactor of mankind who, through the gift of fire, renders man more powerful while also bestowing on him the gift of wisdom, technical knowledge, art and physical speed. Pandora's myth once again refers to the creation of the perfect human being, while her box contained all kinds of ills for man. In the classical period, Lucretius claims that all men, beyond the gods, must reflect perfection.

Science-fiction has continually addressed topics related to the improvement of mankind, its mechanization and biological modification. Today, these are surpassed by the reality of the *"savior sibling."*

In August 2012, a visually impaired Canadian tourist having dinner in a fast-food restaurant on the Champs-Elysées in Paris was wearing a digital eyewear device. The piece of technology used for filming and sending the data to his brain enabled him to see. The man was evicted by the restaurant's security staff on the grounds that he was violating French privacy laws by filming the inside of the premises. However, this eye gear essentially was an extension of this individual's humanity. This leads us to address the issues surrounding trans-humanism and post-humanism.

Three contextual dimensions of responsible innovation

At this stage, three axes of interrogation are being derived to better identify the responsibility of the innovator:

- The environment and ecosystem;
- Technology and politics; and
- The living and its avatars.

These three questions are all linked to one central issue: the individual's spiritual ability, in other words his ability to work his mind and spirit in addressing a specific issue.

• *The environment and ecosystem[4]*

World population stood at one billion in the 19th century, two billion at the beginning of the 20th century and six billion at the start of the 21st century. Since 1975, one billion inhabitants are added every 12 years. Yet, the planet is finite: the resources it produces are limited. How will all these individuals manage to feed themselves and live together? The dates of shortage for raw materials currently used consistently in production processes have officially been determined. In 2010, the European Union classified 14 raw materials such as antimony, beryllium and cobalt, as being of critical importance for saving critical supply sources for the industry. All innovations linked to new technologies use rare earth minerals. Individuals campaigning in favor of a policy for photovoltaic cells seem to forget how environmentally harmful it is to produce these, as it draws on these rare earths. The Toyota Prius, a hybrid car which enables lower fuel consumption, also uses these rare minerals. Moreover, the uneven distribution of the latter can potentially lead to major geopolitical issues.

One third of energy is used to produce energy. In 2010, global energy consumption increased by 5%; China becoming the largest consumer. Is it right to criticize a developing country's decision to not make environmental issues and concerns a top priority? Is it right to tell a Chinese man that he can do without a refrigerator? What would be the consequences

---

[4]Pavie, X (2012). *Innovation responsable: Stratégie et levier de croissance des organisations.* Paris: Eyrolles.

if the households of even half of the 1.3 billion Chinese people were to be fitted with a refrigerator? Greenhouse gas emission rates would naturally increase, contributing further to global warming. From 1996 to 2008, 11 out of 12 years were recorded as the hottest, since 1850. Not forgetting sea pollution or even deforestation, producing billions of tons of CO_2 emissions. Out of the 40,000 identified and recorded species, 16,000 are threatened with extinction. This number represents one out of four mammals, one out of three amphibians, two out of three plants and one out of eight birds.

All of these phenomena are complex and human behavior was most likely a contributing factor. The lobbying budget of the oil industry tripled at the Copenhagen Summit! At the same time, some groups claim that all theories surrounding global warming are a pure sham. Very few people know of the International Union for Conservation of Nature. Yet, many hear of the highly publicized views opposing global warming theories.

• *Technology and politics*

We, as human beings, have a constant desire to go faster; our innovations are proof of that. Zero Emission Hyper Sonic Transport (ZEHST), the supersonic rocket plane project by European Aeronautic Defence and Space Company N.V. (EADS), could reduce travel time from Paris to Tokyo to just two hours and a half. Airplanes, nowadays, have capacity for 800 people, illustrating our constant search for the infinitely large. At the same time, research is also pushed towards the infinitely small: researchers are now able to work nanotechnologies and nanoparticles.

In parallel, the desire to control and monitor individuals is also on the rise. This is nothing new, as the English philosopher Jeremy Bentham introduced the idea of the *Panopticon*[5] in the 18th century; a space organized in such a way that a single man could supervise and control a number of them. Today, 65,000 cameras are continuously filming London and its inhabitants every move and Facebook now represents over one million subscribers.

Eighty types of files are recorded in France, 45 of which are illegal. In recent news, the American government asked Twitter to pass over information and data belonging to the participants of the Occupy Wall Street movement.

---

[5]Bentham, J and Bozovic, M (1995). *The Panopticon Writings*, pp. 29–95. London: Verso.

We are constantly controlled and supervised, through a phenomenon already identified by the French philosopher Michel Foucault in 1975: the notion of "Biopower." We are prescribed vaccines that we must receive, the condoms that we must use, the five fruits and vegetables that we must ingest, the walking time that we must cover every day. This translates into the attempt to create what the German philosopher Herbert Marcuse referred to as the "uni-dimensional man," by imposing a normative ideal, prescribing a way to be and think as well as producing the individual. This also takes us back to Aldous Huxley's premonitions in his famous work "Brave New World" and those of George Orwell's in "*1984*." This issue is, evidently, intimately linked to innovation and responsibility.

• *The living and its avatars*

It is nowadays possible to reconstruct and implant a face, as well as most organs. The neurosciences are accessing the most intimate knowledge into the way the brain works. Cloning animals has now become a reality. We are tipping into a world where we will be able to reproduce the living, or simply repair it, implant it, use it as material for medication. It is even possible to create life from fully inert elements, through biochemistry. Science-fiction is after all late in comparison to all that mankind has achieved and learned to do.

Spiritual capacity, cornerstone for thinking responsible innovation

The three dimensions presented can only be deployed appropriately through spiritual capacity. The latter, however, is very complex. If we take a look at an illustration of this complexity within an organizational context, we can see that the main concern nowadays is to take care of employees on a personal basis. Programs promoting a healthy work/life balance, aim to essentially protect the employee from an intrusion of professional life into an intimate setting. Once the individual is home, he should no longer have to think about work. This, nonetheless, has another more devious consequence: when the individual finds himself at work, he should not think about his private life. He should focus on the growth of his organization and therefore innovate, at the risk of forgetting about the society he and his firm are operating in. However, who are these innovations intended for? Are they not the very element that should make him responsible as a citizen?

The innovator is not an individual like any other. He has the ability, through his innovations, to change the face of the world, whether on a small or large scale. Consequently, the work of innovation cannot limit itself to the professional sphere. It is an intimate process continually at work within the innovator, at all moments and all occasions. In this sense, it is therefore not favorable to create a clear separation between the innovator's private and professional life.

We cannot foresee the consequences of innovation or the impact of the launch within a new context. The issue does not concern our ability to do something, but rather our willingness (or lack thereof) to do it. An improved knowledge base regarding the living, along with a decreasing influence from the Church, which once prohibited any intervention on the living means that we are now willing to take risks and experiment more, we are playing at alchemy.

What is the solution to guarantee a responsible innovation? The answer can be found in *Winnie the Pooh*, which begins as follows:

> "Here is Edward Bear, coming downstairs now, bump, bump, bump, on the back of his head, behind Christopher Robin. It is, as far as he knows, the only way of coming downstairs, but sometimes he feels that there really is another way, if only he could stop bumping for a moment and think of it."[6]

Christopher Robin could take his bear in his arms or jump from the top to reach the bottom of the stairs. However, he prefers to come down the stairs by letting Edward Bear's head bump off each step, in the same way that we hit the planet with our actions.

Doing things, differently

It is important to understand that we are not trying to undermine innovation. On the contrary, remaining competitive is absolutely essential, along with making profit in order to survive and keep investing. We have to keep "coming downstairs," but can we do so differently? This is the very essence of responsible innovation. How can we do things differently, and still do them as well?

We are not talking here of social or societal innovation, which would, for instance, consist of helping the poor or the disabled. Responsible innovation concerns innovation in the broad sense, which distinguishes it clearly from an organization's corporate social responsibility (CSR) or sustainable development policy.

---

[6]Milne, AA (1926). *Winnie-the-Pooh*. London: Methuen & Co. Ltd.

1

THE EMERGENCE OF THE RESPONSIBLE INNOVATION CONCEPT

1. An Explanation of the Terminology

What is responsibility? What is innovation? What do they mean for organizations? In order to understand responsible innovation, each one of the term's component parts must first be clarified. These questions lie at the heart of this chapter and can be understood through a better understanding of the roles and implications of the three actors who stand at the intersection of these two key concepts: individuals, managers and companies. From the outset, we can see that these actors are in fact complex composites: a manager is also — and first and foremost — an individual and a company is composed of a group of managers. The key question analyzed here is the different interactions between them, the transformations that blur the understanding of the stakes and roles which they each occupy in society. An individual becomes an employee, who becomes a production tool for a company. How is he then responsible? Towards whom? For what? What are the limits of this responsibility? When does it apply?

Common agreement is that innovation follows invention, where invention is the discovery of something new. Myers and Marquis (1969) provide a definition on innovation which perceives the concept of innovation not as a single action but rather as a total process of interrelated sub-processes.[1] Following this definition, innovation is concerned with commercial and

---

[1] Myers and Marquis (1969) define innovation: "Innovation is not a single action but a total process of interrelated sub-processes. It is not just the conception of a new idea, nor the invention of a new device, nor the development of a new market. The process is all these things acting in an integrated fashion."

practical application and it covers a process in which intellectual thought is brought into practice by means of various sub-processes such as testing and prototyping, reflection on its added value among customer groups. In his book "Innovation Management," Paul Trott[2] follows this line of reasoning and states that innovation is equal to the theoretical conception plus technical invention plus commercial exploitation. That is, innovation rests upon the basic invention which needs to manifest in a commercial activity and provides value (financial, social or environmental) to the organization. Based on the inclusion of these perspectives, Trott[3] defines innovation as:

> "Innovation is the management of all the activities involved in the process of idea generation, technology development, manufacturing of a new (or improved) product of manufacturing process or equipment."

Innovation, then, can manifest in various ways. Joseph Schumpeter[4] was among the first to provide a comprehensive view on the typology of innovation. He argued that innovation is not only about physical change but can also manifest in terms of processes and organizational forms. Therefore, his concept of innovation covers the introduction of a new good, a new method of production, the opening of a new market, the conquest of a new source of supply of raw materials, and the introduction of a new organization. Trott[5] builds on this typology and discusses the changes in various ways (see Table 1).

These innovation typologies provide direction of how responsible innovation can manifest as well. Following Table 1, we suggest that responsible innovation may be associated with each of the types of innovation. Despite the many surveys and market studies undertaken by companies prior to market launch, the innovation environment is defined by its uncertainty, making its success impossible to predict. The need by companies to minimize the uncertainty of success drives many organizations to research ways

---

[2]Trott, P (2012). *Innovation Management and New Product Development*. New Jersey: Prentice Hall.

[3]*Ibid.*

[4]Schumpeter, J (1954). *Economic Doctrine and Method*. New York: Oxford University Press. First published in German in 1912.

[5]Trott, P (2012). *Op. cit.*

Table 1. Types of innovation.[6]

Type of innovation	Example
Product innovation	The development of a new or improved product
Process innovation	The development of a new manufacturing process
Organizational innovation	A new venture division; a new internal communication system; introduction of a new accounting procedure
Management innovation	TQM (Total Quality Management)
Production innovation	Quality circles; Just-in-time (JIT) manufacturing
Commercial/market innovation	New financing arrangements; new sales approach
Service innovation	Internet-based financial services

of filling this gap, with the aim of reducing the possibility of failure following launch. However, most innovators do not consider the consequences of the innovation beyond economic success while innovations that pose social and environmental pressures are often bound to fail as well. This very uncertain feature gives rise to the stakes of responsible innovation, whose essence is to question the consequences of an innovation. The management of complexity in responsible innovation is then governed by various steps in the innovation cycle. These are the leader's strategic vision, the management of policy and talents, the corporate culture regarding innovation, technology, the evaluation of performance, the communication and success and the timing of innovation and implied risks (Figure 1).

In particular, the time issue is crucial and refers to the moment when an innovation is launched at the most favorable time to be accepted by customers. Researchers have referred to this as the problem of sinking and missing the boat.[7,8] On the one hand, sinking the boat happens when the innovator enters the market too early and various flaws such as technological robustness or misunderstanding by the customer and stakeholders are

---

[6]Trott, P (2012). *Innovation Management and New Product Development*, 5th Edition. Harlow: Pearson Education Limited.

[7]Mullins, JW, Forlani, D and Lerner, J (2005). Missing the boat or sinking the boat: A study of new venture decision making. *Journal of Business Venturing*, 20(1), 47–69.

[8]Dickson, PR and Giglierano, JJ (1986). Missing the boat and sinking the boat: A conceptual model of entrepreneurial risk. *Journal of Marketing*, 50, 58–70.

Figure 1.   Analytic prism of dynamic innovation for creating value.

detrimental to the innovation success. On the other hand, missing the boat occurs when the innovator is too late and the window of opportunity is closing. Many times this is a result of quarrelling over questions such as *"Have we spent enough time on testing the product or service and checking all hypotheses to guarantee it is 'responsible' in terms of society?"* It is this very trade-off between the fast market entry to gain short-term benefits (such as market share and profits) and the responsibility to take care of society and prevent negative impacts in the long-term which responsible-innovation deals with.

Different perspectives exist regarding what responsibility is, differing across disciplines and business sectors. Jeff Ubois (2009),[9] provides a useful

---

[9]Ubois, J (2009). Conversations on innovation, power, and responsibility, p. 52. Available at http://beyondradiation.blogs.com/mblog/2010/02/index.html. Accessed on February 12, 2010.

framework highlighting differing approaches to the concept of responsibility, across various sectors such as law, economics, engineering and design.

- In law, responsibility is framed in terms of liability, or proximate cause. A key question would be, if innovation builds on the work of multiple actors, how is responsibility shared among them, and who is ultimately responsible when something goes wrong?
- In economics, it is framed as externalization of costs, risks and moral hazard. To the extent that innovation creates risks, how can they be measured and assigned, particularly when there is potential for irreversible consequences?
- Engineers and medical professionals may operate under codes of ethics or practices that address responsibility.
- Designers have searched for answers with "user centered" approaches, and argue that responsibility can rest with the end user.
- To other researchers and scientists, responsibility in innovation means avoiding liability, protecting subjects of research and addressing issues of agency and unintended consequences.

Adapted from Jeff Ubois.[10]

2. Exploring the Notion of Responsibility

Whether you are an employee, a citizen, an association, or a company, the notion of responsibility is complex, not only because it involves others, but also because it forces different dimensions to structure themselves around each other within one individual, an individual who is both a citizen and manager.

It has previously been mentioned that the notion of responsibility is linked to the notion of being held accountable for one's actions. Yet, an individual cannot be held accountable for his actions if he himself is not totally free to control them. For example, in an economic context in which the labor market is tense, employees are not totally free to accept or reject certain prerogatives imposed by management.

Even if we cannot be free and independent within civil society, to what extent are we free in our professional life? As managers, is it possible to

---

[10] *Ibid.*

maintain the responsibilities that, as citizens, we must accept? The hierarchical structures, the administrative and operational organization of companies can difficultly articulate themselves around the total freedom required for true responsibility.

a. *Permeability between the private and public spheres*

It is in this context thus, that the question of private vs. professional sphere arises, for innovation in general and innovators in particular.

For several years now, western companies — and governments — have relentlessly been promoting the need for a clear separation between professional and personal life, the famous "work/life balance." Their declared goal is to ensure that individuals are not troubled in their personal life by their professional life. At the same time, however, a possible consequence of this philosophy is the risk of an unawareness or voluntary denial of the impact of one on the other. In other words, expecting a manager to be a citizen who does not think about work, implies that it is also expected of him to strictly limit himself to his professional life when he is at the office, i.e. that the manager gives up his "citizenship" when he enters the building. Among other consequences, this dichotomy entitles managers to act, first and foremost, in the interest of the firm and not in the interest of society. Indeed to what extent do managers wonder: "I have here an innovation which could be successful and thus good for the firm, its success could even earn me a promotion. Should I give up on it because it has negative impacts?" This leads to a disparity between power, concern and care, which leads to possible conflicts for the manager. How can this question be answered? Should managers base judgment on their personal values? Their moral standards? Yet, values and moral principles are very difficult to determine in a universal way.[11] Asian and African standards of morality are very different, and for example, moral sensitivities between men and women also vary widely themselves.[12] The most significant innovations in today's world transcend borders, continents and genders. The manager/citizen dichotomy should be explored in a new light. Should we advocate for a separation between

---

[11]Schwartz, MS (2005). Universal moral values for corporate codes of ethics. *Journal of Business Ethics*, 59, 27–44.

[12]Laugier, S and Paperman, P (2008). La voix différente et les éthiques du care. In Giligan, C (Ed.), *Une voix différente*, pp. III–XXIV. Paris: Flammarion.

manager and citizen to be maintained, or, on the contrary, should these two roles be better accepted and apprehended to ensure that one does not dominate the other?

Innovators must not only understand that they are also citizens, but also that the professional sphere exists to protect the private sphere. Responsibility within the context of innovation has yet to be defined in a way that takes into account all these actors, and their different roles. This responsibility should strive to consider all those the innovation may reach, be it customers, citizens, potential customers, etc. The innovator must not only understand that he is also a citizen, but also, and maybe more importantly, that the professional sphere is there to take care of the private sphere. As Empedocles argued, "there cannot be a human community fair and living in harmony if its members do not think and behave like members of the superior community of living beings."[13] In other words, innovators must remain citizens, individuals working for the good of society and the community of which they form an integral part.

b. *The imperative of responsibility*

The interaction between the private and professional spheres is expressed through the interdependence between manager and citizen, between innovators and innovation-benefiters, where finally, private and public spheres merge. To be a responsible manager, one would need to split himself in two, think as a manager and a citizen: "would I, citizen, support the action that as a manager I am about to implement?" That is the essence outlined by Hans Jonas in his eponymous book, *Imperative of Responsibility.*

In this central book,[14] Jonas questions humanity's right to even exist. If the answer is yes, then it is essential for mankind to adopt a new behavior towards the world, a more caring one. But the question then is: how can this behavior be adopted? How should managers take it into account? And maybe even: with what kind of manager? We firmly believe that innovators must be the cornerstone of this responsibility. As will later be discussed, when interviewed, managers' responses demonstrate that responsibility for them is reduced to the levers on which they can act directly, and more

---

[13]Cf. Balaudé, JF (2010). *Le Savoir-vivre philosophique*, p. 117. Paris: Grasset.
[14]Jonas, H (1979). *Das Prinzip Verantwortung-Versuch einer Ethik für die technologische Zivilisation*. Frankfurt: Suhrkamp. (In German.)

precisely elements tied to the operational nature of their mission. Innovation, however, is a full part of these levers. As they themselves state, innovation is a real actionable lever of responsibility. This statement is both worrying and encouraging: if innovators have that kind of power on society through their new ideas, they are also those who can "change the world" by integrating a responsible dimension to their projects.

Jonas argues that we should not give in to a blind movement of never-ending and unquestionable progress for the sole reason that progress in itself should never be stopped. The use of ethical thinking surrounding the principles and effects of progress and developments could serve as a means of releasing intellectual freedom with regards to the techno-science movement.[15] Jonas strongly values the role of ethical committees, international conventions, legislative debate as well as the importance of raising awareness in schools, engaging in dialogues with actors, such as researchers and doctors, who are clearly responsible for society. We need to fight against automatically adopting a logic of "the established fact" and instead prefer a logic of "a fact previously agreed upon".[16] The never-ending progress of technology has become a threat to both nature and human beings. This gives rise to the imperative of responsibility.[17]

Through the *Imperative of Responsibility*, Jonas suggests providing the future political system with a set of indisputable ethical principles, to serve as support and guide public decision. He argues that this can only happen through the involvement of institutions and democratic exchanges between the government and its people. This will ensure the mediation between ethical principles and their political application.[18]

c. *The responsibility of the citizen/individual*

The notion of responsibility is complex to understand, because it is often associated with concepts such as ethics, moral standards, respect and awareness. However, responsibility has a clear and precise definition. The term "responsible" comes from the Latin word *respondere*, which means "to

---

[15]Pommier, E (2012). *Hans Jonas et le Principe Responsabilit*. Paris: Presses Universitaires de France.
[16]*Ibid.*
[17]Jonas, H (1979). *Op. cit.*
[18]*Ibid.*

account for decisions." This notion can be directly linked to the origin of the concept of civil liability: "any human act that causes damage to another obliges the one by whose fault it occurred to repair it.[19]

To take responsibility for one's actions is to own them, to recognize oneself as being their author. As a consequence, this notion is intimately linked to a question of psychological maturity. This leads, for example, to the creation of the expression "responsible but not guilty," for somebody who kills another in a moment of madness; or for parents who are held responsible for the actions of their children due to the latter's lack of maturity. Responsibility, thus also covers a moral dimension, as indicated in its definition: "the moral obligation to repair a fault, fulfill an obligation, to accept the consequences of one's actions." As a consequence, there is a fine line between responsibility and freedom. Indeed, being free means being able to answer for one's own actions. Being responsible means being held accountable for them, precisely because of this freedom. That is why a truly free man will take on as little responsibility as possible, because it will be difficult for him to assume the obligations deriving from it.

It is important to underline that, in English, three different notions cover the notion of responsibility: responsibility, liability and accountability. The latter is important as it introduces the notion of obligation to "answer to." To a certain extent, this extends the scope of responsibility to include boards of directors, the press and the public. In that sense, all these actors become interlocutors the firm must answer to. Responsibility is thus no longer individual, it becomes shared and versatile. In fact, innovation must be thought around these new constraints and the multiplicity of possible responsibilities. The multifaceted character and versatile connotations of responsibility, as is the case in English, is not without consequence. In a global economy, the notion of "responsible" does not mean the same for everyone, and this can easily generate misunderstandings on what must be done, and how one must act.

d. *Political responsibility*

While Foucault argued that the notion of concern for the self in modern times is to be maintained, it is important to note Hadot's contribution which suggests substituting the antique notion of self-concern or care for the

---

[19]French Civil Code, Article 1382.

more current concept of responsibility.[20] This corroborates teachings from the Stoic school of thought, which underline the dichotomy between those things which depend on us and our actions and those which do not. In other words, what am I responsible for? Having emerged from the end of the 18th century, the term "responsibility" is quite recent and, as with the notion of care, is linked to the concept of power balance. Furthermore, in the same way that care and ethics are linked, responsibility depicts a relationship, not only with oneself, but also with another person. However, as clarified by François Ewald, although responsibility and ethics were perfectly linked at the beginning of the 19th century, the dimension joining these two concepts disappeared the moment responsibility became legalized. The separation of the notions of fault and responsibility which resulted into the latter becoming a tool for assessing risks more than a regulative principle of behavior also led to "relieving each act of responsibility".[21]

From then on it was accepted that "responsibility without fault tends to lead to the weakening of responsibility." In this sense, Engel argues that this applies both before and after the act of making a decision. In the case of the former, it translates into an imposition of liability, without taking the behavior of the individuals being held liable into consideration. It therefore acts as an anesthetic and numbs the action, thereby producing a feeling which is completely opposite to that of responsibility. Once the decision has been made, responsibility without fault does not identify the mistakes which may have been committed and therefore essentially "destroys" the feeling of responsibility as the person who pays compensation for the fault may openly declare that it is not their fault.[22] It becomes clear that the substance of the subject's responsibility both for himself and for the others has been lost.

Responsibility loses its moral dimension through designation from the victim's point of view, which enables the latter to unload onto another person what has happened to them. At the same time, the culprit avoids having to bear this responsibility, which then becomes somebody else's concern. Everyone tries to avoid responsibility. This notion of responsibility

---

[20]Hadot, P (2001). La philosophie comme manière de vivre, p. 149. Paris: Albin Michel.

[21]Ewald, F (1996). Histoire de l'Etat-Providence, (Folio), p. 86. Paris: LGF.

[22]Engel, L (1997). Réguler les comportements. In Ferenczi, T (Ed.), *De quoi sommes-nous responsables?*, pp. 11–36; 80–89. Editions Le Monde.

actually allows completely condemnable actions to be carried out without guilt: "responsible, but not guilty." The idea of a contemporary notion of self-concern seemingly starts with a responsibility for oneself, for others, but which echoes the concept's Latin etymology *"respondere,"* which encapsulates the notion of being held accountable for one's actions and the consequences which may ensue from these. It therefore covers a notion of care for the self as well as for others.

As suggested by Gorgoni, it is the judiciary evolution of responsibility which rocks its very essence.[23] Responsibility has a consistent meaning as long as it is an application chosen by individuals for individuals. However, this meaning weakens as soon as it applies to executive organs.[24] According to François Ewald, "what makes us responsible is the fact that we make decisions when we are responsible for others. This dimension cannot be seized by law because law thinks responsibility in terms of norms and of breaking of those norms. Yet we are not completely feeling responsible when we are submitted to norms. The experiment of responsibility begins with making a decision in which norms had no part".[25] This dimension was the one adopted by Pedersen when he underlined the space we implement in responsibility between the "do no harm" and the "do good".[26] The question of submission to norms thus differs from doing good; the latter is defined as going positively beyond norms. To conclude this argument on the concept of responsibility, we wish to outline the impact which the financial crisis has had on making this notion less accurate. From consumer credits to the latest mobile phones, everything has suddenly acquired a "responsible" coating. Following the "green washing" trend, it appears the next one will be the "responsibility washing" trend.

e. *Responsibility: Moral standards and ethics*

As developed previously, the notion of responsibility implicitly involves ethics and morals. It is important however to differentiate them, while being

---

[23] Gorgoni, G (2006). La responsabilité comme projet. In Eberhard, C (Ed.), *Traduire nos responsabilités planétaires. Recomposer nos paysages juridiques*, pp. 131–146. Bruxelles: Bruylant.

[24] Ewald, F (1996). *Op. cit.*

[25] *Ibid.*, p. 11.

[26] Pedersen, ER (2010). Modelling CSR: How managers understand the responsibilities on business toward society. *Journal of Business Ethics*, 91(2), 155–166.

aware that ethics and morals do fall under the same scope. Etymologically, these terms refer, both in Greek and Latin, to the idea of customs. They comply with a set of rules, values, commandments, prohibitions that govern one's conduct.

Moral standards are understood as a normative code that delimits what is "good" and what is "bad." There are thus actions that are moral, and others that are immoral or forbidden. Ethics on the other hand, is intrinsically linked to the acceptance and implementation of the code by the subject.

Therefore, what is understood by Moral standards is a set of rules of action that are offered to individuals and groups through the intermediary of diverse prescriptive apparatuses: family, educational institutions, religions, etc.[27] Morals can thus be understood as the real behavior of individuals with regards to the rules and values offered to them. In other words, the term refers to the way in and extent to which they abide to principles of conduct, prescriptions and interdictions.[28] Moral standards determine how and to the extent to which individuals act with regards to a prescriptive system explicitly or implicitly given in their culture and of which they are more or less aware. This is called "morality of behaviors."[29]

Ethics on the other hand, was well summarized by George Edward Moore as an "enquiry into what is good."[30] However, this notion of "good" is versatile and forces us to wonder what exactly is good. Why? For whom? And how? Ethics is first and foremost based on Greek philosophy. To some extent, Aristotle — but also the Epicureans, Stoics, and some Pre-socratic philosophers — was the first one to introduce the notion of ethics. This notion was always turned towards the enquiry of the status of our values and the actions they entail. Ethics is understood as a theory, an explanatory discourse intended to enlighten our moral intuitions and guide our behaviors. Unlike morals, ethics is not articulated according to a prescriptive apparatus, but according to the way in which each individual constitutes himself a moral subject of the code.[31]

---

[27] Foucault, M (2001). *Usage des plaisirs et technique de soi.* Reprinted in *Dits et Écrits II*, p. 1358. Paris: Gallimard.
[28] *Ibid.*
[29] *Ibid.*
[30] Moore, GE (2008). *Principia Ethica.* Cambridge: Cambridge University Press.
[31] Foucault, M (2001). *Op. cit.*

In that sense, does responsible innovation stem from ethics or moral standards? Neither and both at the same time. It does stem from moral standards insofar as it depends on prescriptive oracles, i.e. companies, legislations, etc., and ethics because it is both in accordance with and dependent on prescriptive elements, and also its own personal convictions or perceptions.

f. *The responsibility of a firm*

The discussion about the responsibility of organizations in society has a long history. It is difficult to trace back who started the discussion, but in a noteworthy search, Archie Carroll[32] found evidence of publications dating back to the 1930s and 1940s, e.g. Chester Barnard's (1938) *The Functions of the Executive*, JM Clark's (1939) *Social Control of Business*, and Theodore Kreps' (1940) *Measurement of the Social Performance of Business*. Since then, various authors have discussed the role of organizations in society and popular management magazines such as *Fortune* committed an article to the subject in 1946.[33] The contributions of various authors led to the conceptualization of the social and economic involvement of companies in 1970.[34]

Responsibility for a firm is just as hard to define as for an individual. The first difficulty of a firm's responsibility is to know where its responsibility lies. Who is responsible for what, how and where? If we understand where a person's responsibility lies towards himself and his environment, it is important to understand where said responsibility lies within a company. Is it at the level of employees? Management? Shareholders and boards (executive, board of overseers, etc.)?

- Companies lie at the center of a system of responsibility which is both shared and sequential. The creation of a company generates a certain

---

[32] Carroll, AB (1999). Corporate social responsibility evolution of a definitional construct. *Business & Society*, 38(3), 268–295.

[33] Carroll, AB (1994). Social issues in management research: Expert's views, analysis and commentary. *Business & Society*, 33(1), 5–29.

[34] Wallich, HC and McGowan, JJ (1970). Stockholder interest and the corporation's role in social policy. In Baumol, WJ, Rensis, L, McGowan, JJ and Wallich, HC (Eds.), *A New Rationale for Corporate Social Policy*. New York: Committee for Economic Development.

amount of accountability at different levels: employees, managers and stakeholders. This constitutes a first level of responsibility. These individuals form a first responsibility chain, and all are linked to each other;

- A second level of responsibility that a company takes on is that of legal person. As such, the company has responsibilities towards society at a large and must, for example, pay taxes, etc. This constitutes the first level of interaction with society in general, and citizens in particular;

- The third component of a firm's responsibility covers its interactions with its partners: suppliers, subcontractors, institutions, etc. The company must be responsible towards its commitments and the contracts it recognizes. The difficulty of this third level of responsibility lies in the fact that legislations are less clear cut. It is impossible to have laws that cover every type of interaction. As a consequence, this can result in a risk of domination of one's over the others; and

- Finally, the last component of this responsibility, which is at the core of our discussion, is the awareness of a responsibility towards future generations. This is all the more complex as in this particular framework, no negotiation is *effectively* possible. If it is true that there are some control organisms created to preserve the future, any actions we undertake are however limited to our current and actual knowledge, and we can only anticipate as best as we can. This last responsibility is much more complex as it is not oriented towards an institution, an organism, a partner or an individual, but towards "somebody" who doesn't exist yet. And this is the responsibility that must be fully accepted by innovators, because when we innovate, we do not know what the impacts on future generations, their attitudes and behaviors might be.

g. *The question of stakeholders*

The different levels of responsibility previously identified demonstrate that the manager-individual and the company are the principal stakeholders. However, this statement should not limit our reflection. Indeed, the fundamental question of corporate responsibility with regards to responsible innovation is to take into account the expectations of all the different players, whether they are internal or external to the company. In this context, stakeholders must be understood not so much as a constellation of actors, but as one, global ecosystem. Indeed, as underlined by Freeman, stakeholders can be seen as "any group or individual who can affect or is affected by the achievement of the organization's objectives,"[35] however, they should also be seen as motors, as contributors to a global system in which nothing can work if one party were to disappear. In ecology, "ecosystem" designates the unity composed by an association or a community of living beings and their biological, geological, hydrological and climatic environment, etc. The elements which compose an ecosystem develop networks which exchange energy and matter, to preserve and maintain life. This also applies in the corporate context: stakeholders cannot survive without employees, and the latter cannot live without suppliers, and suppliers themselves would serve no purpose if it were not for clients, who cannot project any growth without the development of companies that address their needs, and so on and so forth. In other words, we must all worry about the "health" of others because our own "health" depends on it. According to Freeman, this is articulated around three levels:

- "Rational" level, a descriptive approach which leads to an exhaustive identification of all the stakeholders;
- "Process" level, which deals with the systematic processes developed by companies to take into account the interests of all stake holders in its conception, implementation and control strategies; and
- "Transactional" level, which seeks to understand how to interact, negotiate and manage the stakeholders.

Table 2 shows the different categories of stakeholders for any company.

h. *Managers and responsibility*

The first actors of the implementation of sustainable development — more precisely responsible innovation — are managers. Indeed, managers are responsible for the actions taken by the firm.

Managers are at the intersection of the individual and the company, and their role is difficult to define because they are not only citizens in their civic life, they are also the ones who bare — with a group of other

---

[35]Freeman, RE (1984). *Strategic Management: A Stakeholder Approach*, p. 48. Boston: Piman-Ballinger.

Table 2. Different categories of a firm's stakeholders.[36]

Stakeholders			Expectations
INTERNAL STAKE-HOLDERS	Personnel	General Management	• Staff flexibility and mobility • Acceptance by unions of the company's general policy • Staff motivation, social cohesion and attractiveness • Adequate delegation (efficiency of middle management)
		Middle Management	• Consistency in decisions by general management • Respect of the chain of command and adequate delegation (respecting their position as an intermediary) • Involved in general management
		Employees	• Attractive compensation • Good working conditions • Degree of autonomy/personnel development • Training • Company savings scheme • Consideration from their superiors • Social and environmental policy (employees' civic role and development prospects)

(Continued)

[36]Ernult, J and Ashta, A (2007). Développement durable, responsabilité société de l'entreprise, théorie des parties prenantes: Évolution et perspectives. *Cahiers du CEREN*, 21, 4–31.

Table 2.   (*Continued*)

	Stakeholders		Expectations
		Staff Representatives	• Respect social benefits and freedom of unions • Involve employees in firm's general policy • Clarify staff management rules
EXTERNAL STAKE-HOLDERS	Business World	Suppliers	• Respect contracts and prevent anti-competitive practices • Trust and long-term relationship • To be integrated in the production system: purchasing, delays, transport, outsourcing • To be integrated in the quality system • Social and environmental policy
		Clients/ Consumers	• Price • Innovation/product quality/customer service • Environmental and sanitary risks linked to products • Respect regulations (social and environmental) • Product certification (quality, eco-labels, traceability)
		Banks/ Insurances/ Investors	• Share value • Efficiency and transparency of management (governance) • Financial risks (strategy and investments) • Reliability of information and transparency (reliable reporting) • Monitoring and frequency of monitoring (internal audits and management control) • Legal responsibility (transparency)

(*Continued*)

Table 2. (*Continued*)

Stakeholders		Expectations
		• Risks derived from the activity (pollution, internal security) • Certified production system (quality) • Legal certification (audit financial accounts)
EXTERNAL STAKE-HOLDERS	Political World	• Local economic development (local employment, pull factor which will attract other actors from business world, optimization economic benefit on local activity, etc.) • Long-term investment (durability) • Environmental and sanitary risks and impacts linked to the products or activity • Taxes and fees (contribution towards public finances) • Respect regulations • External communication and involvement in corporate life • Certification
	Media World	• External communication (transparency) • Involved with local bodies and institutions • Environmental and sanitary risks and impacts linked to the products or activity • Respect regulations (social and environmental) • Certification (annual report and quality) • Involvement in and respect of local life

(*Continued*)

Table 2. (*Continued*)

Stakeholders	Expectations
Residents and NGOs	• Involvement in and respect of local life • Environmental and sanitary risks and impacts linked to the products or activity; public nuisance (sound pollution, infrastructures) • Respect regulations (social and environmental) • Legal responsibility (transparency)

people — the values of the legal person: the firm. It is them indeed who bear the responsibility in their actions, decisions, and approaches within the firm. It is thus important to examine, in detail, how individuals act, how they understand responsibility, and how they act when the issue of responsibility is at stake.

It is interesting then to attempt to limit the behavior of an individual and the concept of inherent responsibility beyond the complexity of combining professional and private spheres.[37] Several studies revealed that spontaneously, managers, have a narrow conception of responsibility, one that is said to be "mediatic." This can be seen in managers' reactive approach to responsibility, i.e. to do no harm, to concentrate on the risks that can be avoided, as opposed to a proactive approach, which fully understands organizations' potential to transform society.[38]

---

[37]Pedersen, ER (2010). *Op. cit.*

[38]Responsibility is our main concern, however we must often refer to studies on corporate social responsibility (CSR), and will thus regularly employ CSR and responsibility as synonyms, even if there can be slight variations in the understanding of these terms. To that respect, CSR is qualified as defined by the Commission to European Parliament, to Council, and the European Economic and Social Committee (March 22, 2006): "Corporate social responsibility (CSR) is a concept whereby companies integrate social and environmental concerns in their business operations and in their interaction with their stakeholders on a voluntary basis. It is about enterprises deciding to go beyond minimum legal requirements and obligations stemming from collective agreements in order to address societal

i. *Managers and the multiplicity of responsibilities*

To fully apprehend what responsibility represents for a manager, it is interesting to look at a study carried out among one thousand employees on their actions in terms of responsibility at work. This study was directed within eight large companies, and their managers classified the following criteria by order of priority[39]:

- Respect of the environment.
- Being able to supply products and perform services which satisfy consumers, not in terms of needs but in terms of quality and safety. Being able to answer the user–client demand, by supplying the best product or performing the best service to maintain a long-lasting relationship;
- Being concerned with employees' well-being: offer them a safe and healthy work environment; treat them with dignity, respect, inspiration and sense of humor, etc. Allowing them to develop their skills through training;
- Being responsible towards the local community and, on a more global level, society;
- Respect current legislations; and
- Creating value for stockholders and stakeholders: companies must act in the debate on globalization, competitiveness and sustainable development. The primary goal is to generate a benefit for all stakeholders.

The results of this survey show, first and foremost, that the notion of responsibility for managers is quite unclear. More precisely, it involves different dimensions which are not necessarily connected. For managers, responsibility goes from the respect of environment to employee training, their relation to shareholdership, to clients, etc. This brings to light a general misunderstanding of the term "responsibility," different ways of apprehending the term which are the source of many tensions. Indeed, what decisions should a company make if its clients force it to perform actions

---

needs. Through CSR, enterprises of all sizes, in cooperation with their stakeholders, can help to reconcile economic, social and environmental ambitions. As such, CSR has become an increasingly important concept both globally and within the EU, and is part of the debate about globalization, competitiveness and sustainability. In Europe, the promotion of CSR reflects the need to defend common values and increase the sense of solidarity and cohesion."

[39]Pedersen, ER (2010). *Op. cit.* Table II: Key groups of societal responsibilities.

Table 3.   Key groups of societal responsibilities.

Issues	Companies								Total
	A	B	C	D	E	F	G	H	
Respect the Environment	16	82	9	38	61	57	42	46	351
Product Problems									
Supply Products	36	18	4	10	29	30	16	46	187
Product Quality	31	6	0	5	13	12	1	30	98
Product Safety	12	5	2	0	11	14	1	3	48
Product Innovation	25	6	0	1	7	5	3	5	52
User and Consumer Care	33	4	3	5	13	22	5	24	109
Employee Problems									
Employees' Well-Being and Personal Development	20	24	8	30	21	23	6	10	142
Employee Safety and Security	6	40	2	5	41	9	12	14	129
Job Opportunities	3	23	1	6	8	7	3	2	53
Communities and Society									
Community Concerns	6	47	3	10	31	17	15	7	136
Social Well-Being and Development	11	32	1	15	18	18	22	13	130
Social Education	5	5	9	5	3	12	3	0	42
Sponsorships, Philanthropic Actions, Donations, etc.	5	6	0	7	5	12	5	3	43
Legal Conformity	6	20	7	17	17	12	5	11	95
Stakeholders/Stockholders									
Stockholder Concerns	3	18	1	1	10	6	7	6	52
Stakeholder Concerns	1	17	2	2	8	5	10	7	52

which are not environmentally friendly? Which form of responsibility takes precedence over the other? How can the dilemma between social or societal responsibility and provider/client responsibility be solved? (Table 3)

It is also surprising to observe that only few managers mention the notions of diversity, importance, work/life balance, recruitment, human rights, or reducing poverty. Indeed, managers have a very narrow view of

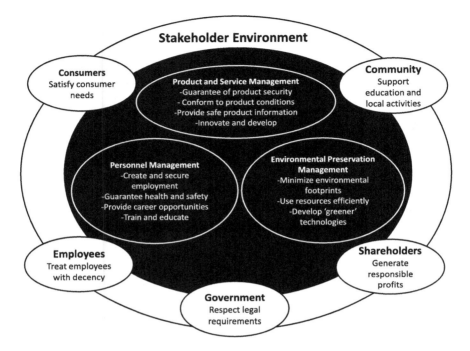

Figure 2. A practitioner-based model of societal responsibilities.

responsibility. This can be explained in part by the fact that they only consider responsibility within their own operational field. They do not imagine that their actions could go beyond their field of competence or defined responsibility. In that sense, they have a classic and "visible" understanding of responsibility: environment, management, etc.

Figure 2 illustrates the areas managers see as areas where they can exert an influence within their company.[40] This representation, designed by Pedersen, demonstrates that managers who are at the intersection of both circles do indeed have a much reduced conception of responsibility. Their main concern is the operational activity of the company, the activities which have a similar mission to their own and that affect them directly. For those reasons, they worry about developing and promoting good quality products/services, in a pleasant working environment which will have as

---

[40]Pedersen, ER (2010). *Op. cit.* Diagram 1. A practitioner-based model of social responsibilities.

little impact as possible on the outside environment (dark circle). There are numerous impacts beyond the operational field, but these impacts are only considered subsequently (wider circle).

This behavior towards responsibility and the poor understanding of its actual definition means that, in best case scenarios, responsibility will limit itself to conforming to the law. The law is the basic reference point, and managers can only turn toward legally-defined frameworks: the law, legislations, market rules, regulatory codes, charters, etc. This does not mean that all managers act this way, or that some do not look for solutions outside of this legal framework. But, generally speaking, responsibility is applied in restrictive ways. While conforming to laws and obligations, managers ensure they "do no harm" and follow the established guidelines.

3.   Is Responsible Innovation Derived from CSR?

The beginnings of the concept of responsible innovation are to be found in the work of philosopher Hans Jonas, whose theories regarding responsibility were discussed earlier.[41] Indeed, he developed the idea that technical knowledge exceeds predictive knowledge and hence considered the adoption of a form of ethics to bridge this gap to be essential. Without rejecting science and technology, Jonas argues that it is necessary to develop a form of responsibility that is fully human in order to face the dangers associated with the rise of technology and which put humanity at risk.

However, despite the fact that they differ in many ways, it is important to understand the exact extent to which the issue of responsible innovation is connected to the question of corporate social responsibility (CSR).[42] For that reason, we will begin with a short detour to explore the emergence of CSR to better understand how it relates to responsible innovation.

a.   *A question of religion*

The question of corporate responsibility is intimately linked to religion in general, and to Protestantism in particular. Max Weber demonstrated the

---

[41] Jonas, H (1984). *The Imperative of Responsibility: In Search of Ethics for the Technological Age.* Chicago: University of Chicago Press.

[42] This chapter is based on the essay by Acquier, A, Gond, J-P and Igalens, J (2011). La religion dans les affaires: la RSE. Available at www.fondopol.org.

crucial role Protestantism played in the development of capitalism.[43] Social responsibility is an issue which was addressed by executives in the US as early as the 19th century through philanthropic activities. One of the cornerstones of this movement was Andrew Carnegie, who in *The Gospel of Wealth* raises the question of the responsibilities of rich businessmen, who he declares owe it to society to lead a less ostentatious lifestyle, and he further maintains that any excess of wealth should be directed towards public interest.

Among Protestants, two notions came into prominence at that time: *trusteeship* and *stewardship*. These notions explore the relationship between the company and society, based on the principle that property is by no means an absolute and unconditional right, and can only be justified if the private administration of these goods can increase the well-being of the community. The defenders of theories around this time included Chester Barnard, pioneer theoretician of the organization of management; Henry Ford, founder of the eponymous group; Alfred Sloan, who managed General Motors for 30 years; and Thomas Edison and Charles Coffin, founders of General Electric Company.

The Catholic stance towards this question was first formulated by Pope Leo XIII and his encyclical *Rerum Novarum*: the wealthy and business owners should not treat workers as slaves; dignity must be respected and it is shameful and inhumane to use men as tools. Leo XIII attempted to build a principle of social responsibility on solidarity, and stressed that managers and employees should not be seen as *de facto* enemies. They are in a mutual relationship of co-dependence: there can be no capital without work, and no work without capital. Pope Pius XI took this discussion further in the *Quadragesimo Anno*, where he declares that workers must receive a fair wage that allows them to provide for their families and to attain to the possession of a certain modest personal fortune. More recently, in *Centesimus Annus* Pope John Paul II addressed the question of ecology, and stated that there is an excessive and disorderly consumption of our planets' resources by mankind. We can see, then, how, by first addressing the question of workers and their relationship to business owners, the Church gradually extended its commentary to business, and its societal role in broad sense.

---

[43]Weber, M (1967). *L'Éthique protestante et l'Esprit du capitalisme*. Paris: Librairie Plon.

The issue of CSR was initially developed in the US for at least two major reasons; the main one being related to the high importance of religion within American society in comparison to France for instance, where Church and State were separated by law in 1905. Moreover, as Max Weber underlined, the protestant ethics, so very present on the American soil, were one of the motors of development of capitalism. Even before the concept of CSR was considered, other forms of social-oriented concerns existed, such as socially responsible investment (SRI), initially carried out by various religious confessions, such as the Quakers. SRI, a valid concern even today, implies investing in companies which conform to a certain set of standards similar to one's own, and thereby excluding from one's investment portfolio any company which acts in ways opposed to one's values: gambling, alcohol, pornography, etc.

b. *The conscience of businessmen*

In 1953, 'Responsibilities of the Businessman' by Howard Bowen introduces for the first time the idea that there is such a thing as corporate social responsibility, which effectively exceeds an organization's strict economic and financial responsibility towards its owners.[44] According to Bowen, the social responsibility of businessmen is based on two principles. The first is the social contract: if a company exists, it is because society accepts it, and in return, the company's actions and methods must respect the laws formulated by said society. The second is morality: through its influence and its decision-making power, a company must have an exemplary attitude that is consistent with the values of the society in which it operates.

For Bowen, the obligation of a businessman is to ensure that the policies pursued the lines of action chosen and decisions made all fully take into account the objectives and values of our society. In other words, their obligation is to place society's collective values above personal values and benefit. This relies on the free will of the businessman himself as an individual, who, according to Bowen, has more power than the common citizen, and as such must thus be capable of understanding the impact of his or her action on society.

---

[44]See Igalens, J and Benraiss, L (2005). Aux fondements de l'audit social: Howard R. Bowen et les églises protestantes. Actes de la 23ᵉ Université d'été de l'Audit social, 1 et 2 Septembre 2005, IAE de Lille. (In French.)

For Bowen, social responsibility must thus be regarded as a tool that helps guide the activity of companies towards reaching the goals that civil society has set for itself.

However, the religious dimension that underpin the structure of CSR did not disappear from the debate, particularly in the US where certain authors suggested that the theorization of the social responsibility of business should be re-orientate towards religion, despite the fact that secularizing CSR would be a more effective way to reach the business world. Responsible-innovation could, in that sense, be the key to this process.

While it is true that religion still has an influence on the question of CSR, the latter is also essentially constituted by a set of texts, treaties and charters all founded on universal secular values: the Declaration of Human Rights (1948),[45] the Rio Declaration (1992),[46] the fundamental principles and rights of the International Labor Organization or the Charter of Fundamental Rights of the European Union (2000).[47] It is in this context that in 1999 Kofi Annan, then secretary general to the United Nations, created the UN Global Compact at Davos, stating that: "I suggest that you, the business leaders gathered in Davos, and we, the United Nations, initiate a global compact of shared values and principles, which will give a human face to the global market."[48]

c. *The secularization of CSR*

The evolution of CSR can be analyzed according to the following chronology[49] (Table 4):

---

[45] UN General Assembly, Universal Declaration of Human Rights, December 10, 1948, 217 A (III).

[46] UN (1992). Doc. A/CONF.151/26 (vol. I)/31 ILM 874.

[47] European Union, Charter of Fundamental Rights of the European Union, December 7, 2000, Official Journal of the European Communities, December 18, 2000 (OJ C 364/01).

[48] However, if it is true these universal principles are shared, or at least seek to be (let's not forget that only 300 French firms signed this pact), the question should not only be discussed and considered at the level of leaders, even if they are crucial. Indeed, the challenge relies just as much on managers who, on a daily basis, are the true decision-makers.

[49] This table was designed by Acquier, A, Gond, J-P and Igalens, J (2011). *Op. cit.*

Table 4. Conceptual evolution of corporate social responsibility according to Frederick.

Concept	Period	Notion and Underlying Program
CSR 1 Social Responsibility of Companies	1950–1960	• Identify a series of moral obligations which companies ought to adhere to. • However, relative difficulties due to the lack of a structured normative platform on which to found these approaches.
CSR 2 Social Receptiveness of Companies	1970–1980	• Focus on companies' instruments and response processes toward demands arising from their environment. • These approaches, while rejecting any normative dimension from the analysis, try to refute the obvious and to legitimize corporate practices without any critical distance.
CSR 3 Social Rectitude of Companies	1980–2000	• The normative dimension re-integrated into the analysis. • Develop a more systematic theoretical foundation (Christian and Judeo-Christian philosophy, Marxism, humanism, etc.).
CSR 4 Cosmos/Science/ Religion	2000 and after	• Separates the concept of a firm's social performance from that of moral crisis. • Displacement of the notion of social responsibility from one centered on the business world to one where corporate/society interaction has a universalistic normative perspective focused on humanity (from corporate to cosmos; social sciences to all sciences and responsibility towards religion). • Religion (understood here as a search for meaning) becomes the fundamental principle of any analysis of the relations between companies and societies.

Source: Table based on Frederick's model (1978, 1986 and 1998).

CSR 1: identified stakes are related to the idea that the interaction between the corporate world and society is in need of adjustments. The notion of accountability is introduced.

CSR 2: the environmental questions are addressed for the first time.

CSR 3: stakeholders are considered for the first time: the individual, the company, society, the environment, stockholders, workers, etc.

CSR 4: CSR becomes the acronym for Cosmos, Science and Religion. This is representative of a shift beyond the limited corporate circle to take into account the global mechanisms of humanity in a very wide sense, including genetic processes, astrophysics, biochemistry, etc. The Cosmos becomes the reference point when dealing with questions of cloning, GMOs, DNA manipulation, etc.

d. *Sustainable development*

The wide-reaching and global formalization of responsibility on the part of companies can be found at the beginning of the 1970s. In 1971, the Club of Rome published the Meadows report *"The Limits to Growth,"* that condemned the over-exploitation of natural resources linked to economic growth. It was the first time that the pertinence of the principle of indefinite growth was questioned.[50] In 1972, the Stockholm United Nations conference on the human environment concluded on the need for an environmental development, "eco-development." In 1980, the French term *"développement durable"* (sustainable development) was coined under the aegis of the International Union for Conservation of Nature (IUCN), alarmed by the gradual disappearance of natural environments.

However, the "advent" of sustainable development goes back to 1987. Indeed, in the report entitled "Our Common Future" (or Brundtland Report, named after the Norwegian President of the Commission, Gro Harlem Brundtland), the World Commission on Environment and Development: Our Common Future (created by the UN) defined the necessary policy to achieve a "sustainable development." The goal of this widely recognized and adopted report was to secularize CSR, in order to make it easier to adopt in managerial economics. The report defined the concept as follows: *"Sustainable development is development that meets the needs of the present without compromising the ability of future generations to meet their own needs. It contains within it*

---

[50]Cf. Ernult, J and Ashta, A (2007). *Op. cit.*

two key concepts: the concept of needs, in particular the essential needs of the world's poor, to which overriding priority should be given; and the idea of limitations imposed by the state of technology and social organization on the environment's ability to meet present and future needs." [51]

"Our Common Future" outlined a set of recommendations that they communicated during the 1992 Rio World Conference on environment and development: "We all depend upon one Earth, one biosphere, for sustaining our lives. Yet each community, each country continues its merry way, anxious to survive and thrive, regardless of the possible consequences of their actions on others. Some consume Earth's resources at a rate that would leave future generations. Others, many more in numbers, consume far too little, and know a life of hunger and abject poverty, disease and premature death." [52]

This report lays the very foundations of sustainable development: one that *"meets the needs of the present without compromising the ability of future generations to meet their own needs."* [53] This initial definition is very clear in its ambitions, even if the term is bandied about and misused here and there. There are a large number of companies which offer so-called "sustainable development" products or services, or build their discourse around this theme, without a clear understanding of the precise definition. However, this unanimously-recognized basis is the starting point from which a sustainable development process can be orchestrated for an organization. In other words, processes to systematically question how the actions undertaken address a specific need while guaranteeing they do not compromise future needs. This balance lies on three pillars that can be summarized as follows:

The Principle of Equity:　— *Provide for all thanks to a better distribution of wealth,*
　　　　　　　　　　　　— *Take into account the southern countries,*
　　　　　　　　　　　　— *Take into consideration an intergenerational equity;*

---

[51] Our Common Future, *Report of the United Nations World Commission on Environment and Development*, presided by Harlem Brundtland.
[52] *Ibid.*
[53] *Ibid.*

The Principle of Prevention: — *Foreseeing and preventing the environmental consequences of a project;*

The Principle of Participation: — *Sustainable development is a collective responsibility which requires an active participation and collaboration from all, at all levels.*

In that sense, simply recycling a bottle of shampoo stamped "sustainable development" does not necessarily guarantee the respect of future generations. It depends on a set of factors, from sourcing, development, manufacturing method, commercialization, development, waste disposal, etc.

The three principles of the Brundtland report are represented in Figure 3 in the form of three spheres, all interrelated, and which together form a whole, i.e. "sustainable development."

An interesting element to mention here is that in France in 2001, the New Economic Regulations included the obligation for listed companies on

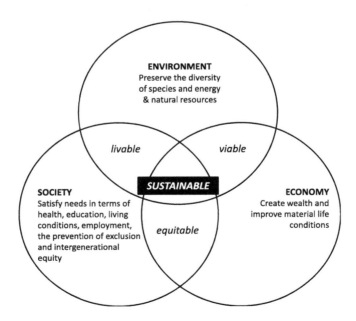

Figure 3.   Principles of the Brundtland report.

the French Stock Market to present an annual report on "the sustainability of their social and environmental performance."[54]

In 1997, sustainable development was extended to managerial spheres thanks to Elkington's notion of the Triple Bottom Line.[55] Indeed, he states that a company must perform in three key areas:

- Economic prosperity;
- Environmental sustainability; and
- Social equity.

This picks up on what the World Business Council for Sustainable Development had previously stated in 1992, when it defined CSR as "the continuous commitment of companies to ethical practices which contribute to economic development while improving the quality of life of employees and their families, the environment as well as society in the broad sense." In 2001, the European Commission supported these views when it declared that CSR, "being socially responsible means not only fulfilling applicable legal requirements, but also going beyond compliance and investing 'more' into human capital, the environment and relations with stakeholders." The European Commission completed this discourse the following year when it stated that "businesses need to integrate the economic, social and environmental impact in their operations."

4. The Understanding of Responsible Innovation

This dimensioning of responsibility is the context in which the concept of responsible innovation is inscribed here. In that sense, our analysis distances itself from the notion of responsibility understood as something social. Indeed, responsible innovation is too often confused with social or societal, or even frugal innovation. These terms are generally understood as innovations aimed at better apprehending the key issues that the most disadvantaged populations must face. For example, such types of innovations include the "little cool," a $70 fridge which operates on battery power, to ensure that fresh produce is not affected by temperature fluctuations in countries where electricity is not stable. The MAC400 electrocardiogram, also

---

[54] *Law number* 2001-420, dated May 15, 2001.
[55] Elkington, J (1997). *Cannibals with Forks, the Triple Bottom Lines of the 21st Century Business*. Oxford: Capstone Publishing.

battery-powered, was developed specifically for India, to facilitate access for farmers from remote areas of the country to this type of medical test. Other inventions designed for India are the $2,200 Nano car or a $35 touchpad. One last innovation worth mentioning is one introduced by Tata Consulting Service. Aware of the costly price of laptops in India, they developed an internet-connection system via televisions, thanks to which it is possible to browse the web from a simple mobile phone. These innovations are essential for these populations, and thanks to constant technical and technological progress, social and societal innovations benefit from a very strong growth. However, this is not the primary objective of responsible innovation: it is not to see responsibility as an end in itself. Responsible innovation is not, and should not be, structured around social innovation because responsibility must be present well beyond these questions. The mere notion of responsibility for innovations is not the prerogative of social innovations, quite the contrary. If it is true that there is indeed a significant market for affordable touchpads and "little cool" fridges, they do remain less significant than market "standards." And it is precisely for these "standards" that responsibility needs to be applied, in the design of their final purpose as well as their processes. Let us not forget that a social innovation might not be responsible *per se*: for example, the $2,200 Nano cars pose a major ecological risk in terms of CO_2 emissions since they lack an adequate filter system for exhaust gas.

An inadequate understanding of responsible innovation and its trivialized use are not without consequence, when responsible innovation should in fact be a full part of any innovation strategy and development. When amalgamated with social questions, responsibility may be relegated to questions that, even if they are essential, are not a part of the daily issues of the competitive, globalized economic world we live in. In other words, the ambition of responsible innovation is not to take on social issues nor to find ways to face social challenges in an innovative way, but rather to become a part of the innovation processes of organizations at a global level in order to gauge the question of responsibility in different sectors and levels: industry and services, high-tech or basic manufactured goods, etc. Moreover, responsible innovation is not limited to certain population segments; it must be considered at a global level, taking into account all targets: young, less young, wealthy and less wealthy, urban or rural, European or Asian, etc.

In the English language, the term responsible innovation is understood in a broad sense, combining questions of responsibility as a whole with social questions. As René Von Schomberg, European Commission

Directorate General for Research, Governance and Ethics unit, stated: "Responsible research and innovation is a transparent, interactive process by which societal actors and innovators become mutually responsive to each other with a view on the (ethical) acceptability, sustainability and societal desirability of the innovation process and its marketable products in order to allow a proper embedding of scientific and technological advances in our society."[56] His analysis includes the social end-purpose of innovations, as well as the innovation process as a whole.[57] These specifications allow us to identify three dimensions of responsibility with regards to innovation:

- Responsible innovation, defined by the European Commission as a transparent and interactive process by means of which social actors and innovators must interact and work together in line with given opportunities, to ensure that societal ethical stakes are preserved;
- Social innovation, defined by the Bureau of European Policy Advisers (BEPA)[58] which must simultaneously answer social needs and nurture new social rapports; and
- Inclusive innovation, aimed at delivering high-performing products, processes and services at a very low price for poor people, from accommodation to transport, medicine to computers. Above all, these innovations must be affordable.[59]

Social innovation does exist, that is an undeniable fact. The goal of this type of innovation is to improve the environment, protect mankind's well-being or working conditions. Social innovation is also aimed at caring for populations which are most at risk. However, let us remember that responsible innovation in this particular context is different. Indeed, its objective is to integrate measures throughout the innovation process as a whole, from conception to market launch, to preserve the environment (non-polluting materials, selective sorting of waste, recycling, etc.), and also consider its

---

[56]Von Schomberg, R (2010). What is responsible research and innovation. Available at http://ec.europa.eu/bepa/european-group-ethics/docs/activities/schomberg.pdf.

[57]Available at http://ec.europa.eu/research/index.cfm?pg=org&lg=fr.

[58]Available at http://ec.europa.eu/bepa/index_fr.htm. Connecting Commission policy-makers with those parts of society is the first and foremost mission of the BEPA; these are new ideas (products, services and models).

[59]Declaration by Dr. Mashelkar, RA during the World Bank S&T Global Forum, December 2009.

impacts on social and economic dimensions. Responsible innovation therefore also includes an awareness of direct and indirect impacts on the user, stakeholders and society as a whole. More precisely, it should consider direct and indirect impacts on social, economic and environmental factors. In this particular context then, innovation is not *per se* research exclusively directed at addressing environmental challenges, human health and working conditions, but rather at conducting an innovation project, in any sector, which integrates all of these dimensions throughout, regardless of the nature of the innovation.

These distinctions are essential: while it remains truly important to generate innovations with a responsible, social and societal finality, integrating responsibility within innovation processes as a whole is much more crucial, because responsible innovation as we have defined it concerns all existing and future companies, regardless of their sector, location, size, etc. To illustrate this concept, let us look at some examples. If Apple were to implement an internal recycling program for iPods, and employed handicapped people or people in great difficulty that need to reinsert themselves into active life specifically for that purpose, then, this recycling program would have an innovative and responsible component. The same could be applied to Grameen Bank who pioneered innovative micro-credits for the very poor.

These two innovations both have a social goal.[60] Yet, we would qualify as responsible an innovation which, in the case of iPods, would not consist in extracting rare earth minerals from Chinese soil to produce toxic products which may pose a major health risk for workers as well as customers. In the case of the Grameen Bank, what seems essential is not so much the goal but the method: where does the money come from? Is there a risk of over-indebtedness for contractors?

Indeed, even if it is a positive thing to integrate people with disabilities into social life, as is facilitating access to loans for the very poor, this should not be at any cost. Most importantly, it is essential to know how to concentrate the responsibility efforts on what will have the highest impact on society and is determining in the innovation process as a whole, for example, to avoid using harmful products, implement upstream measures for recycling, etc.

---

[60]This name is derived from their geochemical properties. The rare earth minerals or "rare earth elements" spread very unevenly across the planet.

a. *Linguistics*

The term "responsible innovation" is no longer keeping pace with its meaning, too unclear and trivialized. As well as having a passive and defensive coloration, it does not allow to point out the particularities of its object precisely enough, thus, remaining of little use. The issue which arises at this stage of our reasoning is the possible impact of lexical variety on the difference of understanding. In fact, there are three English words that are associated with the idea of responsibility: accountable, liable and responsible. The first one has an accounting etymology; it expresses the duty to account for one's action, to tell about it if asked. The second one has a legal etymology; it expresses the notion of a debt related to one's actions and its consequences: if one's actions are damageable to someone or have some negative outcomes, it is one's duty to compensate this. Last but not least, the word responsibility comes from responder (to take the oath) and refers to authority, duty and moral commitment. Responsible is much more used when talking about "feeling responsible," to express the being in charge of something. English people thus, use an expression which does not really take into account the dimension of "accounting for" which yet best describes "responsible innovation."

On the contrary, in French, the three dimensions above-mentioned are all implied by the word *"responsable"* which makes the concept of *"innovation-responsable"* much richer but also more vague than in English. Thus, *"responsabilité"* indeed involves the notion of 'accounting for one's action," but when used with innovation, it has an understood meaning much nearer to the meaning of "being in charge." In Dutch, the concept of responsibility follows closely the meaning of accountable, liable and responsible. These differences and ambiguities of what responsibility means in various languages may lead to misinterpretations when it is discussed among people of different nationalities and languages. The words used are the same but may not fully reflect the vital dimensions of the concept.

2

THE UNCERTAIN NATURE OF THE INNOVATION ENVIRONMENT

1. Deciding in the Unknown and Unknowable

a. *Losing control of innovations*

Determining responsibility requires both being able to understand and to integrate the future, yet without a clear notion of what this future might bring. That is where the difficulty lies. Throughout life, we are surrounded by a constant uncertainty, both in our private and professional lives. Yet paradoxically, it is our awareness which prompts us to act.

The last 15 years have only accentuated the abyss of uncertainty which surrounds us. To better understand the context, we simply need to put some recent examples into perspective, which not only show a certain lack of anticipation, but also plunge us into uncertainty about the future.[1]

The great success of the development of mobile phones was foreseeable. Few people however had gambled on the development of short message service (SMS). The first commercial message via SMS was sent on December 1992; today more commercial SMSs are sent every day than there are people on this planet. The availability of this technology and its affordability generated massive distribution. So, while it took radio 38 long years to reach 50 million owners, mobile phones only needed 13 years to reach the same number of individuals, the Internet only 4, Apple's iPod only 3, and having reached 50 million users in just 2 years, Facebook now represents a database of over 1 billion contacts. This is not to mention Twitter's whopping increase in the number of active users from 30 million in 2010 to more than 218 million in 2013.

The technological race is by no means decreasing. Speculations suggest that, by 2049, a computer with the same computing capacity as all living species put together, will cost less than $1,400.

---

[1]These elements were drawn from research carried out by Fisch, K, McLeod, S and Brenman, J. Available at www.lps.k12.co.us/schools/arapahoe/fisch/didyou-know/sourcesfordidyouknow.pdf.

However, while acknowledging that the Internet represents a technological innovation, it would be nothing without its associated services. Let us not forget that in 1984, there were barely a couple of thousands of Internet services. By 1992, this had reached a million, and by 2008, a billion. This in turn has an influence on lifestyles. For example, in 2008, in the US, one married couple out of eight had met on the Internet.

In terms of employability and education, it is important to know that the 10 most significant job offers in 2010 were for positions that did not exist in 2004. Higher education institutions dedicate five years to preparing students to jobs that have not yet been created. If we take into account that technological information doubles every two years, half of what an engineering student can learn in four years at school is already obsolete in their third year. The employability of every single person and their flexibility are now the key, given that one employee out of four will leave his or her job after one year, and that one out of two will leave it before he or she has completed five years. As information is continuously multiplying and being shared ever more widely across the world, we are faced with concerns beyond storage: the increasing difficulty with regards to ensuring full data and privacy protection.[2]

These few examples serve to underline the uncertainty of our future, of innovation and its impacts. They shed light on a major issue: the loss of control. Indeed, we develop products and services and encourage behaviors, without really measuring the consequences — which, by definition, is difficult, given the uncertainty of an innovation — but more importantly without being sure that we have done everything we can to control these developments. Yet it is precisely this capability to control and manage innovations that will allow us to qualify whether an innovation is responsible or not.

b.   *An ambiguous life cycle*

The challenge then is to know how to limit, insofar as possible, this notion of "uncertainty," the underlying principle at the heart of this discussion. In other words, the challenge lies in identifying and paying special attention to the moments of greatest uncertainty in the life cycle of a new product. Knowing that, the more the life cycle is under control, the broader the scope of responsibility will be, since the end of life of a product i.e. its elimination, destruction, etc., should also be anticipated.[3] In this sense,

---

[2]Cukier, K (2010). Data, data everywhere. *The Economist*, February 25 Issue.
[3]MacGregor, SP and Fontrodona, J (2008). Exploring the fit between CSR and innovation. *Working Paper*, IESE CBS, Barcelona.

if a good understanding of the life cycle of a product or service is first and foremost destined to forecast sales, necessary communication, customer retention, etc., it would also be a valuable tool for responsible innovation.

When the point of view of responsibility is integrated into the life cycle of a product, a "maturity path towards true CSR-innovation integration" is orchestrated, i.e. a path into which the responsibility of the innovation will be integrated. This is crucial to foresee uncertainties, that is to say gaps, "cracks" or "unhooking" in the foreseen curve of the life cycle. The fundamental element then is this chasm, which is what makes our innovation uncertain, due to two factors which have a significant influence on its diffusion: mass media and opinion leaders. The example of Facebook, that we will analyze in more detail later (cf. p. 55), is a typical example of an unforeseeable gap that was not adequately controlled. Mark Zuckerberg never anticipated the hundreds of millions of connected users. The overwhelming success of his innovation exceeded his previsions, and he found himself at the head of a massive database that now imposes a responsibility on him that he had not imagined or desired at the beginning.

Diagram 1 illustrates the gap that exist between early adopters and the others. The challenge for a truly responsible firm is to anticipate this gap, through a global vision. In other words, a company can develop a product it launches onto the market by anticipating the responsibility process

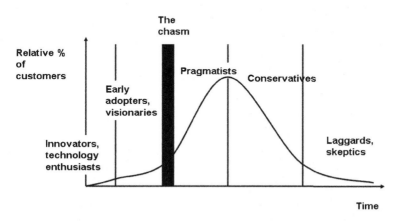

Diagram 1.   Crossing the gap in the innovation diffusion curve.[4]

---

[4]Moore, GA (1999). *Crossing the Chasm*. New York: Harper Collins Publishers.

as a whole, i.e. traceability of suppliers, analysis of carbon consumption, product recycling, taking into account social impacts, etc. However, what the chasm brings to light is that given the unforeseeable character of innovation, everything that was taken into account no longer remains valid. If the success of the innovation goes beyond expectations, further questions will arise, such as, will the supplier still be able to supply in a responsible manner? Will the carbon footprint be affected? Will the recycling processes always be identical? Will employees be able to absorb higher output rates? If the innovation fails, what should be done with the unsold stock? Has a recycling process been planned? If so, what is it? What future will the employees have?

By essence, innovation is directly linked to uncertainty. However, it is not so much a matter of taking into account the uncertainties, as it is actually anticipating all possibilities, successes, failures, non-anticipated uses, etc. And this is what is meant by "maturity path towards true CSR-innovation integration," i.e. how responsibility should be integrated within the path that the innovation will follow.

i.   *3M case study*

With a turnover of nearly $27 billion, the 3M Company is one of the most innovative companies in the world. It files about 600 patents per year, thanks to constant research and innovation. Some of the most famous ones are Scotch Tape, Thinsulate synthetic fiber, the famous Post-its, or its repositionable adhesives for babies' diapers. 3M is also a recognized innovator in business to business schemes, thanks to its Electrical Wire Connectors systems, Microflex circuits or l'Aldara Cream, etc.

Pollution prevention pays

3M has always had to confront the risk of launching polluting innovations, environmentally unfriendly both in their production and consumption, all the way through to the elimination phase. In 1975, this problem was at the heart of the concerns of 3M managers. Their responsibility strategy was built around the concept that the best way to be responsible was to integrate these questions within the development process. 3M thus introduced the 3Ps: Pollution Prevention Pays (Country). This program focuses on impacts on the environment, natural resources, health and safety. The idea was to transform an environmental constraint into a competitive advantage.

This program has been amended a couple of times to take into account more recent scientific and technological discoveries. In 2002, it was integrated transversely, and all levels and categories of staff were included in the program: logistics, transport, packaging, etc. The originality of this program also lies in the fact that it is volunteer-based. In other words, it helps raise awareness that decisions and innovations at any level could have a possible impact on society. This program also involved the range of existing products. By recognizing that prevention is economically sound, the 3P program is designed to anticipate and prevent possible pollution. This program is designed to encourage responsibility so as to eliminate possible sources of pollution by redefining processes, equipment and recycling.

The volunteer involvement of employees in this project is capital for 3M and to demonstrate the commitment of management, the company created an evaluation committee (which has received more than 7,500 projects since 2002, across all possible divisions) which grants Awards to innovations which respect the 3P strategy, namely to eliminate or reduce pollution, reduce power consumption, etc.

Life cycle management process

3M understood that the responsibility of innovation is directly linked to mastering, insofar as it is possible, the products' life cycle and the vocation of its management policy. This is based on wanting to identify and minimize the environmental impacts of the products throughout their life cycle through four criteria: environment, energy/resources, health and security. These criteria are considered in relation to operational processes and investments: equipment acquisition, R&D operations and production operations. But what is extremely original, is the integration of the constant evolution of consumer needs and the uses they make of products within the very process. This dimension enables the company to anticipate the life cycle and constantly adjust the possible negative impacts not only for society, but also for the company.

The life cycle management process guarantees that the company's interest for environment, energy/resources, health and security is respected in the four phases of a products' life cycle: design, manufacturing, use and disposal. This process is carried out prior to the launch and designed to foresee and follow the evolution of the innovation. Therefore, should a problem arises in one of the relevant lines of action (environment, energy, health, security), the difficulty is automatically detected at the level at which it occurs, and can be appropriately addressed. That is when the 3P strategy comes into action. On an existing product, the program will lead to a reformulation of the process, etc.

This comprehensive monitoring process is integrated into the manufacturing processes. 3M's toxicology and regulatory affairs services endeavors to:

- Analyze and optimize every product launched throughout its manufacturing process and in the chosen formulations, improve the product and ensure minimum impact on the environment throughout the life cycle of the product;
- Ensure that products once marketed and distributed are used correctly, providing as much information as possible on the handling instructions to the end user or guiding clients through the customer service; and
- Ensure as much visibility as possible on the way waste material is processed at the end of the products' life cycle.

Some recent 3M products developed within this responsible innovation program include:

- *X-ray film debris recycling process.* 3M developed an innovative film used as a base material for medical imagery, created to avoid any use of chemical products during the development. In the same field, a team from South Carolina and Alabama created a way to recycle residual blue polyester along with "clear" material. Two years after the implementation of the innovation, nearly 20 tons of debris were reused.
- *A water-based adhesive designed to respect the environmental needs of clients.* Furniture companies asked 3M how they could make their glue more environmentally friendly in the manufacturing process of their products. In response to this demand, the Adhesives Division created an international team specially dedicated to developing an easy to use water-based adhesive, that ensured that, as much as possible, environmental criteria is respected to the greatest extent possible. An entirely new product was created, thanks to a brand new technology. This product is a positive advance for the environment, as it consumed between 135,000 and 180,000 liters less of solvent in its first year compared to traditional adhesives and significantly facilitated waste treatment.
- *Halogen-free wire insulation.* Every year, hundreds of millions of computer cables are sold throughout the world to connect computers, monitors, printers and other electronic devices. These wires, as many other insulation elements, are made with halogen containing fluoride,

chloride and bromine. A team of the Connection-Solutions Division successfully designed a halogen-free insulation that works with the same characteristics.

- *Safer cleaning products.* 3M has always strived for an adequate management of the use of chemical products according to the firm's policy, at a comprehensive level. 3M developed a window-cleaning product that, unlike its competitors, does not contain any alkylphenol ethoxylates.

3M's strategy in terms of responsible innovation is clear: to answer needs, to be pro-active regarding its own developments, to constantly improve its own range of products. The company also seeks to be a link in the responsible-innovation chain, for the companies that wish to develop a genuine policy of responsible innovation. 3M does not, however, hide its ambition: adopting a responsible policy is just as much about being capable of developing strong competitive advantages to answer clients' needs as it is about leaving competitors behind.

This example helps us see the extent to which being responsible in innovation requires a policy involving every level of the organization and needs specifically-designed tools, etc. By following this strategy, 3M established itself as a key player, and its clients do not hesitate to request the company's advice or to involve them in their R&D.

2. Adapting Sustainable Development Concept to Address New Global Issues

The social, economic and environmental landscapes facing Brundtland at the time she introduced the principles for achieving sustainability, differed widely from the ones we face today. A series of factors, including political changes which transformed nations, innovations which redefined social norms and limitless scientific progress, including the evolution of DNA structures and the booming development of nanotechnologies, to name but a few, have contributed to the full reshaping of markets and society as a whole. New issues are raised in the modern climate, which cannot be addressed through the pillars of sustainability alone.

The Brundtland report was suited to the society at the time it was issued in the late 1980s, however, it does not include a specification of the final objectives of innovation nor the strategic aspects and consequences involved. Both factors are critical and can no longer be overlooked in the current environment.

While Brundtland's theory focuses on achieving sustainable development, responsible innovation addresses new issues, in light of the highly competitive modern-day climate. New risks posed by the unstable surrounding environment are thereby taken into account, along with the innovative capability of a firm and its integration of responsibility into its operations and innovations, as these are fast becoming the determining factors for survival.

3. The Axes of Responsible Innovation

Three main elements can help us understand what responsible innovation means at an operational level and help identify where measures can be taken.[5] These three axes are the immutable cornerstones of responsible-innovation. Because innovators, as has previously been established, are not employees like others. Innovators are not solely at the service of the company, they are also at the service of the city with all the responsibilities that this entails.

The three inseparable axes of responsible innovation revolve around three major concerns, as illustrated in Figure 4:

- Should every need be met? That is, innovators must question what answers, if any, should be provided to consumer needs.
- As innovators, are we fully aware of our inability to fully assess the extent of the consequences of our innovations (for our clients, our target)? In other words, what direct impacts will our innovations have?
- As innovators, do we know how to identify the consequences of innovations on lifestyles (for society as a whole)? This third axis raises issues concerning the indirect impacts of innovation.

a. *Question the solutions to develop in response to individual needs*

If our inherent nature pushes us to seek constant innovation, it is also because we are constantly dissatisfied. Nothing seems to be able to satisfy our thirst for consumership and ownership. Marketing teams are legitimately continuously working to detect today's and tomorrow's needs and identifying the extent to which these needs constitute a big enough market for investment.

---

[5]Cf. Editorial by Bensaude-Vincent, B (2009). *Colloque innovation-responsable.* Collège de France, April.

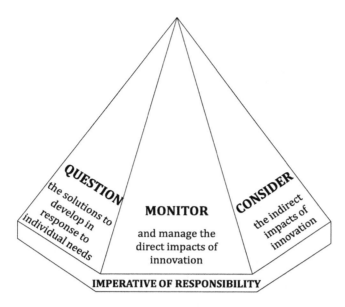

Figure 4.　The axes of responsible innovation.[6]

i. *iPod case study*

Why did Apple develop nearly 20 generations of iPods in less than 10 years?[7] What does that tell us?

From the 'Classic 1G' in 2001 to the 'Nano 16G', Apple continues to flood the market with a colossal amount of incremental innovations: Classic (5G, 10G, 15G, 20G, 30G, 40G, 60G, 80G, 120G and 160G), Mini (4G and 6G), Nano (1G, 2G, 4G, 8G and 16G), Shuffle (1G, 2G and 4G), Touch (8G, 16G, 32G and 64G); not to mention its parallel policy for iPhones (Classic, 3G, 3GS, 4G, 4GS, etc.), iPads (Generations 1, 2, 3, 4 and Air), etc.

If we focus on the iPod, obviously, the insight, the consumers' desire, is still as vivid as it was when Sony launched its Walkman in 1979: the desire to listen to the music we like, wherever and whenever we want. The relative failures of the Digital Audio Tape (DAT) cassettes and the Discman at the end of the 1980s and in the 1990s shed light on the risks involved

---

[6]Pavie, X (2012). *Innovation responsable*: *Stratégie et levier de croissance des organisations*. Paris: Eyrolles.
[7]Apple press release library. Available at apple.com/pr/library/.

in Apple's choice to launch the iPod. However, the success they achieved in merely a few months proved that this desire still existed, yet practically no manufacturer was addressing this insight. Having said that, Apple did not simply seek to meet the "need," and it made no effort to "measure" the potential impact of the launch of its innovations. Instead, building on its technological capabilities, Apple sought to saturate consumers, to incite them to buy the latest model, the one with a click wheel (which was not on the first versions), the one with the biggest storage capacity, the one with a camera, the one that can read videos, the one that will fit in a shirt pocket, and so on and so forth or more recently, the one that can make a phone call. If it is true that there clearly is a technological "gap" in this latest launch, and while we can consider legitimate the development of a product which will allow us to both make a phone call and listen to music, we can question the quantity of intermediary developments. What was their function, if not to shower consumers who only felt the legitimate need to listen to music outside of one's living room and car with products? Competition and innovating for the sake of innovation, progress and performance brought new generations of iPods to the market, but with what benefit? For whom? And at whose expense?

These questions simply illustrate the power of marketing, of innovation and also — and perhaps most importantly — of consumers. It is the interaction between two forms of power that create the situation, and where it is most definitely not the manufacturer who is more powerful than the consumer. It is important to refute the false idea that marketing creates needs. If that were the case, what should be said about some colossal failures, including some by Apple? For example, the first Macintosh laptop (1989), that was a total failure; the ancestor of the iPad, the Newton Pad (1993), that only few remember; or of the PowerMac G4 (2000). Facts confirm that this affects all markets: Renault paid the price of their failure with Avantime (2002), as did Peugeot with its 1007 (2005); Bic's perfume (1988) or even Danone's Danao (1998), etc. The list is endless, however, each and every one of these products benefited from a significant marketing budget, sometimes amounting to millions of euros. If marketing could create demand, then these ideas would still have been translated into innovations, i.e. successes. This goes to prove the fundamental role played by consumers in the success or failure of innovations, and demonstrates that they are far from being simply sheepish buyers, a simplification that many people seem to believe.

While marketing does not create consumer needs, it does detect them, and later translates them into products and services and places them on the market. The role of marketing is thus not to create needs but to place what clients desire onto the market. In other words, and here lies the complexity of our claim: should every detected need always be answered? Should marketing automatically orchestrate everything as soon as a need is detected? Is there not a responsibility on marketing directors, innovation directions to know how to measure these launches? If Apple clearly identified a need, to which the response was the iPod and the iTunes platform, to what extent is it necessary to launch 20 variations of the same product, other than to guarantee short-term profit for its stockholders at its customers' expense? Why was the iPad not launched with all the improvements that iPad 2 had to offer from the beginning? The camera, speed of the processor, etc., were features that had already been developed by Apple when its first version was launched. Technological evolution is an important criterion, but it would be perfectly possible for Apple to offer, updates for a given product for a certain fee, which customers could purchase by simply visiting an authorized store. Instead of flooding the world with 300 million iPods,[8] Apple could just as easily sell updates and thereby limit the proliferation of versions of its products, while still developing its turnover.

That is precisely why the notion of responsibility should also be applied to the marketing of the innovation. To what extent should all needs be satisfied? Is it because high-school students do not want to do their homework that an automated homework online service should be launched?[9] Is it because a portion of the population has questionable sexual desires that special vacations should be organized to satisfy these desires?[10]

Responsibility is also about discerning when new launches should be accepted with caution and how to control them to allow consumers to "digest" them. Responsibility also means taking into considering new production methods so as to consume differently; system updates is simply one example among others.

---

[8]Available at http://itunes.apple.com/fr/podcast/apple-keynotes/id275834665.

[9]*Libération*. Available at faismesdevoirs.com ferme déjà ses pages. March 7, 2009. Cf. Pavie, X (2010). *Management stratégique des services et innovation*, pp. 11–31. L'Harmattan.

[10]See for example the websites: pleasuretours.com; alternativephuket.com; globalfantasies.com; temptation.originalresorts.com; affordable-adult-vacations.com; wildwomenvacations.com; pornweek.com.

b. *Monitor and manage the direct impacts of innovations*

The second axis is the impossibility of innovators to foresee the impact that launches will have on both current and future clients. Indeed, this is directly linked to the uncertainty arising from the implementation of innovations. The mission of any company's marketing department is to forecast sales as accurately as possible, to ensure proper supplies, and an adequate stock management, etc.

The difficulty for innovators to "foresee" is due partly to possible mistakes in market studies. Whether they foresee success or failure, such forecasts remain mere previsions. This discussion has already brought to light the extent to which marketing does not create demand; at most, it uncovers it. The lists of marketing failures also underline the axis of innovation: the inability of innovators to foresee.

To the lists offered previously, we could add innovations which did not meet the forecast success: Sega's Dreamcast (1998), France Telecom's Bi-Bop (1991). On the contrary, client surveys had predicted a failure for the Walkman in 1979, Ikea's proposal in 1947, or for Logan in 2005. Only the tenacity of some managers challenged these previsions. There are countless examples of products that went beyond or did not reach the estimated sales. These erroneous forecasts seem to increase as the race for innovation progresses, with its fast-paced decision making and decisions made in haste to beat competition, sometimes even at the expense of clients' life, like the Ford Pinto,[11] sadly known as the "the barbecue that seats four."

i. *Ford Pinto case study*

In 1968, Lee Iacocca, the President of Ford, decided to launch a new model: the Pinto. The innovation lay in the process: its production phase, with a normal 43 months roll-out, was reduced nearly by half to 24 months. The stylized design of the vehicle was important for the engineers: the decision was taken to make the car lighter — to make it more cost-effective — and, for a more aesthetic final product, the fuel tank was placed at the rear end of the car, to ensure harmonious lines.

---

[11]Shaw, WH and Barry, V (1995). *Moral Issues in Business*, 6th Edition, pp. 84–87. Belmontk: Wadsworth Publishing Company. See also Raymond, J (2003). La Ford Pinto: le contre-exemple américain. *Le Polyscope, le journal de l'École polytechnique de Montréal*, 36, March.

The National Highway Traffic Safety Administration (NHTSA), responsible for enforcing US standards, recommended the company apply the 301 standard: a crash test at 31 mph in order to protect passengers from crash-induced explosion risks due to gas tank leakage. Ford performed the stipulated tests but only three cars passed it. At that time, the 301 standard was not obligatory. So in 1971, Lee Iacocca decided to launch the Pinto in the market.

Studies demonstrated that, out of the 400,000 crash-induced explosions in the US every year, 3,000 resulted in burn deaths, and in just as many serious burn injuries. The NHTSA report estimated that adopting the 301 standard could have prevented 40% of these fatalities.

By the end of 1977, Ford had to face a very high number of lawsuits due to the vehicles' gas tank. The NHTSA decided to examine the Pinto, including previous models and concluded that the obvious dangerousness of the gas tank, namely due to its being placed at the rear end of the car, make it more subject to explosions.

At the beginning of 1978, Ford initiated a recall of all circulating cars — 1.5 million — while stipulating that the company was not in agreement with the findings of the NHTSA. The cost of this measure: $20 million. But between 1971 and 1978, at least 53 people had already found a tragic death in Pinto accidents.

If we take a look back at the decision Ford took in 1971, the company faced a dilemma: should they adapt the new Pinto to the 301 standard as suggested by the NHTSA, knowing that it was not mandatory yet and that implementing it would mean delaying production? Or should it produce the new model regardless of these recommendations, knowing that in the event of an accident, passengers would thereby be exposed to risks at least twice as high? The problem was financial, and opting for the former alternative would leave the door wide open to their competitors in this niche market.

In fact, Ford's decision was based on a report entitled "Fatalities Associated with Crash Induced Fuel Leakage and Fires," carried out by Ford's Director of Automotive Safety, J. C. Echold. This study revealed that implementing the new design which met the 301 standard would represent an extra cost of $11 per car.

These costs were compared to the legal costs the company might face in the event of crashes inducing fatalities or severe injuries. Therefore, the company's estimates were quantitative. According to another NHTSA study, the company would lose $200,000 per casualty. This estimate included: the loss of productivity for the lost years of work ($173,000), administrative fees, compensation for the victim's suffering ($10,000), hospital fees ($1,125), funeral costs ($900), etc.

At the moment of the decision, Ford estimated that it would produce a total of 12.5 million cars. So at $11 per unit, implementing the modifications was evaluated at a total cost of $137.5 million. The losses due to accidents, however, were only estimated at $49 million (according to a prediction of 180 fatalities, 180 serious burn injuries, and 2,100 burnt cars). The difference, thus represented $88 million, and this difference justified the rational decision to not perform the gas tank design change.

Ford was comforted in this decision, in that between 1971 and 1978 the company was acquitted in the 50 lawsuits it faced over that period. Indeed, legally, there had been no wrongdoing on Ford's behalf as the security standards in force at the time had been respected. Obviously, though this was never openly admitted, the company did everything it could to delay the adoption of these new standards by the NHTSA and therefore, their mandatory implementation.

What this case brings to light, is that, even in foreseeable situations, decisions are made, which fail to consider human nature or human well-being. What really matters is the greatest possible profitability, in the shortest period possible. Ever-more virulent competitive situations drive innovators — or decision-makers — to launch their innovations, and to match ever-tighter deadlines. Everyone wants to be the first to launch the latest innovation, and thereby "block" their competitors. A major consequence of this is a higher risk that the innovation might fail, and most importantly, without regard for the impact the innovation in question might have on their clients — human beings. This then is the challenge of the second axis: to understand, accept and therefore anticipate the consequences of any given product or service or another, medium and long-term, on the health or even lifestyle of the end user. As an innovative company, to fully apprehend these elements you must ask: what incidence will my cigarettes or my alcohol have on my customers? What impact might the waves of my network, my high-voltage lines or our latest mobile phone have on users? But it is also means being concerned about the impacts of possible over-indebtedness of financial institutions, of the potential exploitation by websites of personal information, etc. Once more, it is important to address these questions with a certain maturity to know how to go beyond frameworks that are simple, economic and the firm's short-term policies.

c. *Consider the indirect consequences of innovations*

The third and final axis concerns the need to consider the impacts that an innovation might have beyond the framework from which they emerged. In other words, to be fully be aware that we interact with each other, consciously or unconsciously. If the previous axis dealt with the impacts of innovations on clients or users, this third axis accepts not only that an innovation can indeed have an impact on its clients, but also that it can also have an impact on its non-clients. This degree of responsibility requires a certain maturity: to envisage being held accountable to somebody who seems to be outside of the scope of one's actions. This is the debate that arose around smoking in public areas. The things I do not only affect me but they also unintentionally affect my peers. This line of thought therefore, also attempts to understand the meaning of freedom: imposing one's own free choice and freedom to smoke does not mean one understands what freedom means.

However, if we can easily understand the detrimental aspect of cigarettes on others, it is not as easy to make the same calculation for an innovation that is in development. Of course, anticipation is the key here, but it is not always possible to do this in a comprehensive and exhaustive way. Indeed, scientific innovation, as responsible marketing, can lead to a sectorial permeability which cannot always be identified from the outset, in other words, an innovation in a given sector can have an incidence on other sectors.

For example, the consequences of the launch of a new, faster, more powerful plane, but that generates significant noise pollution, should not only be assessed on the aircrew, ground crew and its clients. The pollution also affects residents as well as the whole ecosystem around the airport, facts the French *Grenelle de l'environnement* underlined when it stated that corrective measures should be taken.[12] The same principle applies to cars equipped with air-conditioning, which will consume an average of 15% more than a car which does not have this option.[13] Carbon emissions will not only have an impact on the car driver, but also, for example, on anyone riding a bike near that car.

---

[12] Available at http://www.legrenelle-environnement.fr/Convention-avec-les-acteurs-du.html. We should also note the measures taken to reduce sound pollution to protect the well-being of residents, which also increase aircraft fuel consumption.

[13] Gagnepain, L (2006). La climatization automobile — Impacts consommation et pollution. In *Repères*. Agency for the Environment and Energy Management, Department of Transport Technology.

d. *Cases for responsible innovation*

The three axes we have just introduced provide a basis for achieving an operational application of responsible innovation. They aim to question the responsibility of the innovator with regards to a new innovation project, from the approach used right through to its implementation. The main objective of the following two examples is to provide a better understanding of the various mechanisms orchestrated around each axis.

i. Air-conditioning case study

What answers for what needs?

The process of air-conditioning consists in modifying, controlling and regulating the climatic conditions (temperature, dampness, level of airborne dust, etc.) of a given place for comfort (offices, houses) or technical reasons (medical laboratories, electronic components manufacturing premises, operating theatres, computer rooms).

Making air-conditioning for cars accessible to the general public, answered a clearly identified consumer need: the user of a car wants to drive as comfortably as possible when, for example, the outside temperatures gets high. This invention saw the light of day in 1884.[14] An Englishman had the idea of placing a box with ice on his carriage, between his two horses. With a fan activated by the wheels, the mechanism directed the cold air — in fact ice chips — towards the carriage.

An invention becomes an innovation whenever it finds a market, as soon as it reaches a significant number of clients. In 1939, Cadillac developed factory-fitted air-conditioning in its vehicles.[15] Although it was a little unpractical at the beginning, — the evaporator took up the whole back seat — the system was modernized in 1953.[16] The mechanism works by means of a refrigeration compressor powered by the motor and the evaporator, a system similar to domestic fridges. It was placed at the back of the car, between the back seat and the trunk. In 1957, Cadillac developed a draft-free aeration and ventilation system.[17]

---

[14] Available at http://www.arehn.asso.fr/dossiers/clim/climatization.html.
[15] *Ibid.*
[16] *Ibid.*
[17] *Ibid.*

The inability to foresee the direct consequences of innovations

Obviously, the impact of the implementation of this innovation was not considered at the time: scientific knowledge and especially the understanding of possible environmental impacts or carbon emissions were still in their infancy, so naturally, questions like this were simply not asked. Added to this, in the 1950s, society in the US was oriented only towards progress, innovation and comfort, and conquering new markets, etc.

In its early stages, installing air-conditioning in vehicles was cautious, as it proved to be very costly. However, by the end of the 1980s, such installation became more generalized, and today very few new cars leave factories without this equipment. Air-conditioning is offered as a standard, just as is the choice of gearbox. However, every car equipped with air-conditioning generates 15% more carbon emissions than a car that is not equipped with this option.[18] Statistics[19] indicate that this will cause an additional 39% emission by 2030, generated mainly by cars. Its impact on the environment, our lifestyles, on all citizens, on our daily life[20] is significant.

Health risks

- Air-conditioning systems are known to produce waters which foster the development of pathogenic organisms, such as the Legionellosis, an infectious disease caused by bacteria which grows in natural or artificial freshwater systems, and in organic environments conducive to their development (thermal resorts, air-conditioning systems, etc.);
- Injecting disinfectant products into the air-conditioning systems can lead to health problems, namely the development of chloride-resistant pathogens;

---

[18]Gagnepain, L (2006). La climatisation automobile — Impacts consommation et pollution. In *Repères*. Agency for the Environment and Energy Management, Department of Transport Technology.

[19]Energy Information Administration (EIA) (2008). History. *International Energy Annual 2006*, June–December. Available at www.eia.doe.gov/iea. Projections: EIA, World Energy Projections Plus (2009).

[20]Available at www.arehn.asso.fr/dossiers/clim/climatization.html.

- Air-conditioning systems as a whole are composed by filters which need regular cleaning and periodic changing; and
- By definition, air-conditioning can only exist in a closed space, in which different polluting agents will build up. Regarding the transmission of viruses between different premises via air-conditioning systems, the French Agency for Environmental and Occupational Health Safety has identified the danger of the transmission of viruses between different premises via air-conditioning systems, saying: "In buildings fitted with an air-recycling ventilation system (air-conditioning in office buildings or in buildings widely frequented by the general public such as supermarkets), the risk cannot be excluded, however, it is difficult to assess as it depends on a number of unknown factors (virulence of the virus strain, the way air is spread through the ventilation units and systems, and so on)."[21]

Environmental risks

- Air-conditioning is so extensively used that, for example, energy consumption in France is higher during summer than in winter, all the more so since the 2003 heat wave, which generated lots of attraction around this type of equipment. This is paradoxical because France's current energetic supply (essentially nuclear) cannot provide enough energy, and must sometimes operate at reduced capacity because of refrigeration difficulties[22];
- Air-conditioning depends on refrigerant devices that use greenhouse gases (such as HFC-type gases, which produce 2,000 times more greenhouse effect gases than CO_2), a part of which is rejected into atmosphere, due to accidents, or a bad management of the end of the life cycle of the equipment. Moreover, many air-conditioning devices leak. Disruptions in the air-conditioning circuits of houses, hotels and public places are frequent, especially in very warm countries, dues to thermal choc; and
- There is no provision for gas recovery or recycling for devices and cars which are at the end of their life cycle.

---

[21] Afsset recommendations, June 11, 2009.
[22] Les centrales nucléaires doivent s'adapter aux canicules. dixit. Available at www.notre-planete.info/actualites/actu_326_centrales_nucleaires_adaptation_canicule.php.

This example illustrates the three axes defined previously:

- a growing consumer demand for air-conditioning;
- the inability, in the early stages, to apprehend the consequences;
- it does not only have an impact on drivers, but on society as a whole; and
- there is a sectoral permeability insofar as society as a whole is affected by it.

This naturally leads to a key question: what car manufacturer would offer cars without air-conditioning? And also: who would buy them? Indeed, contrary to these conclusions and despite being aware of the inconveniences generated by this equipment, a considerable number of adverts and discounts promote the option for only a few extra euros when one purchases a car. Not to mention the fact that today this equipment is installed as a standard.

Responsible innovation is particularly relevant in this context; it is thus also about behaviors and attitudes. Cars are, first and foremost, a means of transportation designed initially to help you go where you want, when you want. This consumer insight, with perfectly legitimate primary motivations — need, pleasure, obligation — evolved to the point where it has been diverted from its primary objective: solely being considered as a means of transportation. George Friedman heavily criticized these "nations on wheels,"[23] and chastised an "overuse" of cars due to a general lack of courage, out of selfishness, comfort, and wanting to avoid others. Moreover, the proliferation of options for cars which serve purposes that are neither necessary nor functional, sedan's heated seats or a sixth gear (the inherent power of which is absurd considering regulatory speed limitations) enhance the situation. On the other hand, however, innovations such as anti-lock braking system (ABS) or airbags are crucial.

ii. Facebook case study

The responsibility of an innovator — whether this is someone dedicated to this particular mission, or a marketing person or from of a strategic service — is a question which arises in the industrial sector as-well-as in the services economy. This is all the more important considering new information and communication technologies. Indeed, the Facebook network is particularly affected by questions of responsibility that arose with the

---

[23]Friedmann, G (1970). *La puissance et la Sagesse*, p. 55. Paris: Gallimard.

incredible growth of the social network. Let us look back at this innovation along the lines of the three identified axes of responsibility in innovation.

The need for people to interact online

Initially, Facebook was "just" the fruit of the creation of a Harvard student in his dorm room, who wanted to make his university friendships last, a need obviously shared by the community to which he belonged. Within two weeks, two thirds of the school was already connected to the network. A common need to see, be seen, show, exchange, share, etc. meant that less than three months later, more than thirty American universities were connected to the network Mark Zuckerberg[24] created.

The inability to anticipate all impacts

From its very launch, its detractors pointed out the limitations of this innovation. On the one hand, they warn us about a possible exploitation of private data for commercial use, and on the other hand, there is the risk of intrusion in peoples' private life given the multiplicity of personal questions on religious or politic opinions, sexual preferences, etc. Not to mention the use of the "wall" feature with the intention of harming people, as has happened several times between colleagues, for example.

If Facebook sold the data from its network for advertising purposes or commercialize targeted spaces depending on what the personal preferences connected users declared in their profile, the risks would be manageable and could be anticipated. In other words, Facebook's boss can manage this significant database in a more or less responsible way. The question of responsibility is then known and identified. However, the problem of responsible innovation in the case of Facebook goes beyond these aspects. Being responsible is to guard oneself against uncertainty. What are the risks of a database of nearly one billion connected users being owned by a private company? If they are not clearly identified at present, this does not mean that the situation can be ignored; quite on the contrary, we should imagine hypotheses to forestall these dangers. What are the risks of having a database in one place, managed by a private body?

When we join Facebook, we expose ourselves to risks which are difficult to foresee, because we simply do not know the possible uses of identity theft and identity usurpation and exploitation. The founders themselves

---

[24] Available at facebook.typepad.com/faceblog/histoire_de_facebook.

probably do not have the answer to this question. If we look back at the past there have been various examples of misused registers, for example school registers during the Second World War, that help us apprehend the extent to which there are significant risks in revealing too much of one's identity, and the danger of having so much intimate information stocked in one place.[25]

If the risks cannot necessarily be measured at the beginning of an innovation, can the full extent of opportunities it represents be grasped? After the Iranian presidential election of June 2009, many electors took the streets to express their anger after the defeat of candidate Mir Hossein Moussavi, and protest vigorously against electoral fraud. While these protests are considered by many as the most important ones since the Iranian revolution of 1979, the political power in place sought to take control by deadlocking media, namely foreign media. The Iranian people were thereby deprived of mobile communications and had no access to international news sources. To remedy this problem, Facebook and Google simultaneously announced the launch of a translation service from and to Persian, to facilitate communication between Iranians and the rest of the world. So the day after the election of June 12, 2009, the partisans of Moussavi admitted how they had used the social network extensively during the electoral campaign to promote their ideas.[26] This is only one example among many (the "Arab Spring" revolution of 2011), which came into being thanks to Facebook, and actually became true counter-powers to the powers in place.

e.   *Constructing and de-constructing the innovation process*

It is therefore necessary at this stage to reconsider the innovation process and its impact in terms of societal issues. How can individuals from the marketing profession, the scientific community or even the innovation sector not feel concerned — whether consciously or not — by the common good when going through the following procedure, as illustrated in Figure 5:

- Society and citizens are surveyed in order to detect needs and prospects which are not currently being met;

---

[25] See Black, E (2001). *IBM and Holocaust: The Strategic Alliance between Nazi Germany and America's Most Powerful Corporation.* London: Little Brown.
[26] Available at http://www.numerama.com/magazine/13220-Google-et-Facebook-se-mettent-a-l-heure-iranienne-un-peu-tard.html.

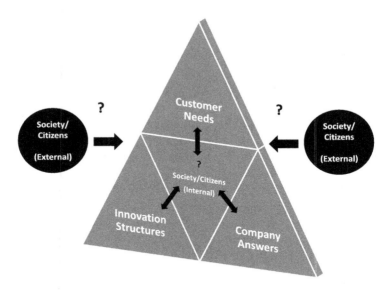

Figure 5.   The alternating role of society in the innovation process.[27]

• Customer needs are then translated by the marketing department. The innovation structures and R&D department are then briefed to find answers to the needs. A solution is formulated and ready to be launched;
• Once again, citizens are involved: as potential buyers.

This sequencing of innovation is carried out without any real consideration for societal issues, which should be discussed, taken into account or integrated throughout the process. The innovator — as well as the citizen — operates in isolation. However, both parties need to interact with each other in order to acquire a better understanding of the key issues at stake in innovation, both from the perspective of the individual who demands the latter and the one who produces it. Responsible innovation first and foremost involves an understanding of the porosity between the company and the citizen. This notion needs to be clearly integrated in order to counter the situation we are currently experiencing: an unhealthy and unsustainable relationship of "who dominates whom" between the company and the citizen, both of which are constantly alternating their roles. This is

---

[27]Pavie, X (2012). *Innovation responsable. Stratégie et levier de croissance des organisations.* Paris: Eyrolles.

triggering "anti-business" and "anti-branding" reactions on the one hand and attempts at controlling customer needs, purchases and consumptions on the other.

The entire elimination of cars in our society seems unimaginable. A constructive collaboration involving the state, citizen and the firm is the only way to encourage the development of vehicles, of transport in general, by innovating and offering new modes of behavior, which is the main idea behind the bicycle sharing system implemented in large cities such as the *Vélib'* concept in Paris.

With regards to air conditioning systems, a termination of the commercialization of such systems could have been agreed upon, following the release of results showing the devastating impacts it causes. An analysis of the *chasm* carried out during the development phase would have showed the need to control the explosion of consumption for such systems. For instance, it could have been reserved exclusively for emergency vehicles, ambulances or even haulage contractors whose quality of work depends on their physical comfort.

At the same time, innovation can also generate responsibility. A gas powered air conditioning system could often be replaced by a mechanical cooling or ventilation system. From their conception phase, buildings should take into account environmental impact by building thick walls with high thermal inertia, for instance. Air conditioning systems can also be replaced with various alternative techniques such as bio heat and cooling systems, adiabatic cooling systems or even ecological air conditioning systems. These work without refrigerant, using solely the evaporation of water. This results in the reduction of power consumption and the continual renewal of air.

Therefore, only the acceptance of a clear porosity between the citizen and the innovation structures can guarantee that one does not dominate the other. The clear and regular communication to citizens would encourage them to become more involved in public debates relating to these issues. However, firms and innovators still need to be convinced to open their doors in order to collect information which could enable them to increase their performance.

3

A GLOBAL INTEGRATION OF RESPONSIBLE INNOVATION INTO ORGANIZATIONS

1. Impact of Responsibility on the Innovation Strategy

a. *A new model for integrating responsible innovation into organizational strategy*

As previously discussed, a responsible innovation strategy can be integrated within organizations operating in any sector. As such, responsible innovation does not only apply to the renewable energies industry or to sustainable chemistry, but rather consists of a method aimed at helping any organization to become responsible through their processes, products and/or services no matter what sector. One of the main elements of this strategy is a process for monitoring impacts of the company or innovation project on social, economic and environmental factors through creating a set of hypotheses throughout the development of the project. These hypotheses will be tested once the project is launched to ensure both previously estimated and unforeseeable impacts are taken into account and suitable action is taken accordingly.

It is clear that the opportunities to create or preserve the most value and the impact of being responsible on short-term costs will vary greatly among industries and sectors. For example, a mining company could significantly reduce its short-term costs through developing innovations that reduce energy and water usage. A clothing retail company could improve resource efficiency through value chain innovations because their biggest impact will be in the raw material and use stages of clothing. An energy company may have greater opportunities to gain value from new products such as through the development and investment in smart grids.

As discussed previously, in his book "The Imperative of Responsibility," Hans Jonas questions whether humanity should continue on existing. If the answer is yes, he argues that the human being should then adopt a new attitude of concern and responsibility towards the world, thereby stating that one should act in such a way that his or her actions are compatible with the preservation of future human life.[1]

This principle ties in with the Kantian maxims concerned with the same issue, such as: "Act that your principle of action might safely be made a law for the whole world,"[2] as well as: "Act in such a way that you treat humanity, whether in your own person or in the person of any other, always at the same time as an end and never merely as a means to an end." The first maxim highlights the obligation to consider potential global consequences and the fact that individuals can share the same concerns interdependently from other individuals. The latter maxim particularly emphasises the principle of responsible innovation, concerned with the preservation of human life. We believe that these attitudes should be the very essence of the innovator's mindset, as he essentially embodies the pillar of responsibility towards the society as a whole. Through his ideas and innovations, the innovator not only has great control over the world, but can also change it by integrating the dimension of responsibility into his or her actions. This represents the cornerstone of responsible innovation.

Figure 6 highlights the relationship between Brundtland's theory, the axes of responsible innovation and Jonas' *Imperative of Responsibility* which are all critical components of the responsible innovation strategy. It provides a framework in order to integrate responsible innovation into a firm's strategy. This ensures that Brundtland's three pillars for sustainable development are not only taken into account, but are also adapted to suit modern day issues, as illustrated through the three axes of responsible innovation.

b. *Adapting responsible innovation to SME specificities*

While many of these business considerations are general across all companies it is important to address the opportunities from a Small and

---

[1] Jonas, H (1979). *Das Prinzip Verantwortung — Versuch einer Ethik für die technologische Zivilisation.* Frankfurt am Main: Suhrkamp. (In German.)
[2] Kant, I (2006). *Fondation de la métaphysique des mœurs.* In: Métaphysique des mœurs, trad. Alain Renaut, Paris: Flammarion, 97–108.

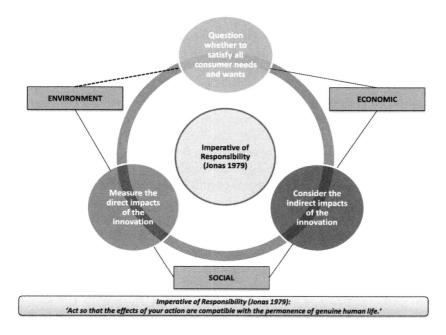

Figure 6.   Integration of responsible innovation into organizational strategy.[3]

Medium-sized Enterprise (SME) perspective. SMEs are considered one of the "driving forces" of modern economies due to their multifaceted contributions in terms of employment, technological innovations and export promotion. While SMEs have great potential, it is well understood that for many SMEs addressing responsible innovation and corporate social responsibility related matters are not driving their agendas. Various valid reasons can be given here, but it is mainly their limited societal exposure which does not pay off to propagandise and publish their efforts with regards to responsible innovation. At the same time, many SMEs consider the regulations about sustainability (ethics, social security, privacy, pollution etc.) as mandatory and restrictive to the entrepreneurial spirit. Consequently, SMEs and entrepreneurs are reluctant to follow standards and formal codes although they do pursue innovations that address grand challenges and provide value to the communities within which they operate.

---

[3] Adapted from Jonas (1979) and Brundtland (1987) (Pavie, 2012; Pavie and Carthy, 2013).

The grand challenges provide significant opportunities such as alternative products and services, new business models and ways of working and more efficient approaches to resource exploitation and energy consumption. Newly emerging technologies may be able to provide substance to pursue the opportunities and solve the concerns of sustainability. However, it requires a more radical approach to innovation, where existing paradigms need to be overcome. Innovators that search for a solution in landscapes more distant from existing ones may also face two other major challenges. One is that of unforeseen developments and, the other, if recognized it may pose moral dilemmas with regards to the implications of the innovation for the sustainable impacts. The problem of unforeseen developments is known as the Collingridge dilemma.[4] According to the Collingridge dilemma, ethical, social or environmental problems can be easily addressed early on during the innovation process where the focus is on the disciplines of sketching and prototyping. However, during this initial stage of the technological innovation process, it will be difficult to have a clear vision on how the technology and its application will be perceived by larger stakeholders groups once exploited in the market. At the same time, once the social, environmental and ethical consequences become more clear at later stages of the innovation process or after market introduction, the development of the technology is often far advanced and the degrees of freedoms have decreased making it difficult to change its trajectory. This requires technology assessment and foresight and inclusion of stakeholders that might be involved once the application is on the market during the early stages of the innovation process. But even if relevant stakeholders are included and the possible consequences of the innovation are fully identified it may pose moral dilemmas for the innovator. The sustainability impacts have a multifaceted characteristic which increase in complexity and interdependencies and, as a result, a solution in one direction, for instance, aimed at increasing the social benefits might be at the cost of environmental impact. Therefore, due to the complex nature and interdependencies among the sustainability impacts the likelihood of success and impact of a solution to solve a specific challenge becomes highly uncertain and projections are difficult to make due to unforeseen side effects. The term "wicked" is introduced in 1973 by

---

[4]Collingridge, D (1980). *The Social Control of Technology.* New York: St. Martin's Press; London: Pinter.

Rittel and Weber[5] to address problems where the effort to solve one aspect of a wicked problem may reveal or create other problems. For the innovator this may lead to moral dilemmas, because solving one problem in one direction may lead to another problem in another direction.

While new technological solutions may be able to increase the social and economic benefits an innovation brings forward without being detrimental to environmental benefits, emerging technologies require a different approach to problem solving which diverts significantly from the way we think about solutions, technologies and application today. The dominant logic, heuristics and current practices to problem solving are not satisfactory since they tend not to break with the existing ones. Exploitation of emerging technologies through established incumbents will put more pressure on the already existing challenge. Established incumbents have existing decision making styles and reward and incentive systems that aim at upholding the current market share and therefore they favor the existing paradigms and states quo.[6] The search for solutions in landscapes which are more distant to the established incumbent poses uncertainty and risk and requires new knowledge which poses problems for established incumbents.[7] Small and new entrepreneurial companies are not hampered by the large installed base, i.e. investments in technologies, production and customers, like large incumbents are and thus are more flexible and take less risk when exploiting emerging technologies. Small and new entrepreneurial companies are also less restricted by formal procedures, existing decision making styles and reward and incentive systems that aim at upholding the current market shares and tend to favor the existing paradigms and states quo as in large established organizations.

Although SMEs are generally unable to frame innovation debates or create significant market opportunities through their own activities, it is worth noting that there are a number of characteristics of SMEs and SME

---

[5]Rittel, HWJ and Webber MM (1973). Dilemmas in a General Theory of Planning. *Policy Sciences*, 4, 155–169.
[6]Christensen, CM (1997). *The Innovator's Dilemma. When New Technologies Cause Great Firms to Fail.* Harvard Business School Press.
[7]Henderson, R and Clark, K (1990). Architectural Innovation. The Reconfiguration of Existing Product Technologies and the Failure of Established Firms. *Administrative Science Quarterly*, 35(1), 81–112.

owner/managers that provide significant opportunities for responsible innovation. These characteristics include:

- Personal values and mind-set of the owner/manager;
- Ability to adapt quickly, if resources allow;
- Less hierarchical organisational structures;
- Engagement in open innovation through supply chain or regional support;
- SMEs can also easily address some niche markets less addressed or not addressed and neglected by larger companies; and
- They have a proximity with users and other stakeholders that could be easily used to identify opportunities.

SMEs are highly dependent on the skill level of their workforce and they have less flexibility regarding the regional supply of a skilled workforce. This is one area that universities can support SMEs in innovation and responsiblle innovation. Given their small resource base, policy-makers can help firms to find the right partner or contact within the university or R&D institute depending on the specific needs that the firm has.

It is understood that innovation in SMEs involves interactive learning and that cooperation is necessary for the competitiveness of SMEs. Because of this, many SMEs regularly innovate through interaction with the wider innovation system. These interactions with other SMEs, universities, research institutes and other intermediary organizations can occur on a regional, national or even transnational level. A pre-requisite for SMEs investing time, effort and financial resources to these arrangements is that they recognize the added value. This spatial dimension to SME innovation will depend on the existing knowledge (of SME and intermediaries) and specific competence needs. In this instance "competence needs" can include technologies, skills or other business functions. This type of transnational innovation process is seen more regularly in R&D intensive and science-driven (e.g. Nano and biotech) SMEs. In summary, Table 5 identifies several benefits and barriers for SMEs engaging in responsible innovation.

This framework will be supported by a simplified code of practice for SMEs that includes all the key issues they need to address. This RI code of practice will facilitate benchmarking and continuous improvement on RI and builds on some characteristics which are specific to an SME:

- the sustainability benefits of new products, processes and services;
- the sustainability impacts of existing products, processes and services;

Table 5.   Responsible innovation benefits and barriers for SMEs.

Key benefits of responsible innovation for SMEs	Key barriers to responsible innovation for SMEs
1. Improved potential to attract new business.	1. Absence of immediate incentives.
2. Improved employee and customer attraction, trust, loyalty and retention.	2. RI direction/definition for stakeholders unclear.
3. Improved supplier's belief in the company's integrity.	3. Lack of collaboration with regional and transnational research institutes/universities.
4. Improved supply-chain engagement (e.g. codes, monitoring).	4. Lack of resource (finance, capabilities, qualified staff) within the enterprise.
5. Cost savings (e.g. eco-efficiency).	5. Insufficient or restricted access to existing subsidies and fiscal incentives.
6. Proactive compliance with legislation.	
7. Enhanced relationships with investors who pursue reduced risk investments.	6. Existing regulations and structures not incentivizing RI.
	7. Transition and technological lock-ins (e.g. old technologies and infrastructure).
8. Improved relationships with government, regulators and local communities.	8. Limited access to external information and knowledge regarding RI.
9. Improved alignment with the values of the owner/manager.	9. Limited access to well-developed RI support services.

- customers' (latent or unmet) needs and the benefits their offering brings to customers;
- global and technological trends;
- behavior of the competition;
- the intentions and needs of intermediaries (distributors and resellers);
- risk management;
- stakeholder needs/expectations; and
- acceptability of the innovation and whether it is reasonable for society.

2. Five Stages for Becoming a Responsible and Innovative Organization

"Responsible innovation is an iterative process throughout which the project's impacts on social, economic and environmental factors are, where possible, measured and otherwise taken into account at each step of development of the project, thereby guaranteeing control over, or at least awareness of, the innovation's impacts throughout the entire life cycle. In the case of impacts which are not accurately measurable prior to the launch but are considered to potentially become critical risk factors once the project is on the market, a number of hypotheses should be formulated in order to be tested post-launch to determine whether the product should be re-integrated into a previous step of the process for amendment aiming to minimize negative impacts."[8]

This chapter introduces five stages for integrating responsibility at all levels of the company. This complete organizational integration ensures that responsibility does not only apply to the production of goods and services but is rather an integral part of the organization and its strategy. A company applying a responsible approach to its innovation process only, could dangerously be considered to engage in "green washing." While the discussion of the following five stages is sequential for the purpose of understanding, the latter are naturally more dynamic in practice, with forward and backward loops taken if necessary and variable time frames for each stage.

a. Stage 1: *Comply with the law*

Legal obligations naturally make up the first step of the organization's journey to responsibility. The central challenge lies in examining the legislation to detect any potential obstacles to the development of innovation. For instance, existing concepts regarding intellectual property and the laws that regulate it in the specific country in which the product would be introduced should be analyzed to ensure any unintentional infringement is avoided. In summary, the aims of this stage is to "Do Good" before the others and therefore gain a competitive advantage by being the first one to innovate on an aspect which will later concern all of the market players. In order to do this, the company needs sufficient knowledge and legal expertise to

---

[8]Pavie, X and Carthy, D (2013). Responsible-innovation in practice: How to implement responsibility across an organization. *Cahier Innovation & Society*, No. 33.

anticipate rules and regulations. Consulting a professional firm on this topic could therefore be the best way to ensure the organization gets accurate and up-to-date legal information. The company would also need to get involved in co-opetition with other market players to create solutions.

For instance, a co-opetition project in the financial sector could be initiated by a financial consultancy company. The project could be structured around a working group, consisting of several banking institutions, insurance companies and academics, aiming at addressing legal current and upcoming issues which are specific to that sector. An outside moderator would guide the debate constructively and ensure that the targets are met. This would also serve as a basis for achieving the second stage of the process, i.e., Anticipating future legal requirements.

The series of ongoing lawsuits between Apple Inc. and Samsung Electronics regarding the design of smartphones and tablet computers began with Apple issuing an official complaint in April 2011 accusing Samsung of "slavishly" copying its design. By August 2011, Apple and Samsung were litigating 19 ongoing cases in nine countries; by October, the legal disputes expanded to 10 countries. By July 2012, the two companies were still embroiled in more than 50 lawsuits around the globe, with billions of dollars in damages claimed between them.

Amazon was said to infringe on patents related streaming and routing media with its Instant Video service as per Single Touch Systems claims. Amazon Instant Video allows customers to rent or purchase content from its film and TV catalogue, which boasts 120,000 titles, of which thousands are available to prime subscribers at no additional cost. Single Touch R&D owns a portfolio of 18 issued and additional pending patents related to mobile search, commerce, advertising and streaming media. Some of these protected concepts are at stake in its dispute with Amazon.

b. Stage 2: *Anticipate future legal requirements*

This second step of the model introduces the notion of staying one step ahead of legislation by anticipating future legal requirements. The purpose of law enforcement is to be in sync with the state's expectations for innovation and therefore be able to anticipate and formulate regulations which become an opportunity for innovation. The firm should develop more effective foresight in the area of innovation by using horizon scanning and risk analysis techniques. Horizon scanning encompasses a range of web-based approaches for identifying emerging issues or opportunities, such as innovations, associated impacts, risks and benefits, by scanning the emerging literature and then synthesizing it through knowledge management approaches. Problem formulation is the initial, qualitative phase of risk assessment that defines who might be at risk, what they may be at risk from and which specific areas should be assessed in the subsequent phase of quantitative risk assessment.

By anticipating future legislations, the firm remains the first to innovate on an aspect before it becomes mandatory for all market players, therefore gaining a major competitive advantage. An example of this can be seen in the ready-to-wear clothing industry. In 2011, Greenpeace launched a campaign called Detox focusing on toxic chemicals used in the textile industry. The NGO denounced the use by the textile industry of harmful substances like alkilphénols, perfluorocarbons and phthalates, used for purposes like dyeing clothes. These dangerous substances pollute the environment around the production areas (in China, Mexico, etc.), and can harm the user by causing itching, allergies, and even disrupting the hormonal system. Even though it is still legal to use toxic substances in the manufacturing of clothing, 15 ready-to-wear brands including Zara, Mango, Esprit, Levis, Uniqlo, Victoria's Secret and Benetton have joined hands with Greenpeace and are working towards eliminating hazardous chemicals from their supply chains and products.

c. Stage 3: *Think the value chain as an ecosystem*

In the third phase of this process, the organization needs to improve efficiency at all levels of the value chain, especially in terms of its suppliers. It is necessary to build a value chain where all of the actors and organizations involved are oriented towards responsibility. Natural resources and services that were previously not taken into consideration should be evaluated and quantified at this stage from an economic point of view. This would include redefining the operations to reduce water and electricity consumption, emissions and waste. A product with a negative impact on the environment is generally cheaper than one which is eco-friendly, due to the fact that the higher cost to the environment does not translate into higher price to the customer. Quantifying these external costs and including them into the product price would make the environmentally friendly item more competitive in terms of price while at the same time enabling the company to invest in sustainable innovations. Intertek has developed a Green Leaf Mark certification to provide an indicator that a product has been independently tested and found to conform to multiple existing environmental regulations.

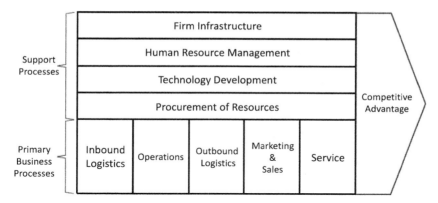

Figure 7.   Porter's Value Chain.[9]

By using Porter's Value Chain[10] as a tool, see Figure 7, we can establish how to re-design primary business processes and support processes in order to integrate responsibility along all of the firm's individual activities.

Primary business processes are made up of all inbound and outbound logistics, operations, marketing and sales and service activities. Regarding the degree of responsibility of its inbound and outbound logistics activities, the firm could evaluate the impact of transport on CO_2 emissions and traffic congestion. It could then re-organize these activities to minimize the negative impacts. In terms of operations, measures could be deployed to reduce energy and water consumption in the production process while monitoring waste and carbon emissions. Workers' safety should be optimized while the use of dangerous substances if necessary should be closely supervised to minimize any risks. Integrating the concept of responsibility into the firm's marketing and sales activities could involve ensuring that consumer information and privacy is respected. Keeping the consumer in focus, it could also mean eliminating price discrimination or introducing special rates for those consumers considered to be financially unstable. Shifting the focus to the market as a whole and the actors operating within it, it could also mean preventing anti-competitive pricing practices. Integrating responsibility into after-sale service activities could involve an efficient management system for

---

[9]Pavie, X and Carthej, D (2013). *Op. cit.*
[10]Porter, M (1985). *Competitive Advantage: Creating and Sustaining Superior Performance.* New York: Free Press.

all consumables such as engine oil or ink cartridges. Furthermore, the firm could introduce a system of responsible elimination for all obsolete items.

Support processes cover all activities concerned with the firm infrastructure, human resource management, product and technology development and the procurement of resources. In this way, responsible practices could be applied to the types of methods used for financial reporting and the application of government measures to increase transparency across the firm's management system as well as its legal and financial activities. The organization should also review its human resource policies to ensure that these are in line with responsible values. This includes optimizing training and staff health and security measures, while promoting diversity and eliminating discrimination issues in the workplace. Product and technology development activities could incorporate closer collaborations with universities to carry out academic research on ethical practice topics, such as animal testing or GMOs and liaise back with the firm, providing guidelines on how to be more responsible. Ensuring products are user-friendly and safe while providing ease of access to recycling methods at the end of product life would also enhance the firm's sustainable practices. The conservation of raw materials would also apply to this category and would need to be reviewed thoroughly in light of the upcoming shortages of certain major materials. The purchasing policy would need to be examined to ensure that the procurement process and use of natural resources are efficient and sustainable.

A good example of this is IKEA. In June 2011, IKEA UK announced an initiative to improve sustainability which involved switching its entire company car fleet to low emission hybrids. The program follows steps already taken by IKEA to reduce energy consumption, cut emissions and to source products from sustainable suppliers IKEA has committed to reduce CO_2 emissions worldwide by 9% by 2010. In the first phase of the hybrid vehicle initiative, IKEA UK announced that it would purchase up to 50 Honda Civic Hybrid cars from the Japanese carmaker with further deliveries later on. The Honda Civic Hybrid offers industry leading fuel consumption of more than 60 miles per gallon and CO_2 emissions of $109\,g/km$, significantly below the Europe Union's ambitious target of $120\,g/km$. Honda was the first car manufacturer to bring a Hybrid car to the mass market.

d.   Stage 4: *Develop responsible products and services*

The fourth stage of the model is about creating, designing, developing and launching responsible products onto the market while monitoring and managing the impacts of these products on social, economic and environmental criteria throughout the entire life cycle.

In order to develop a sustainable supply of raw materials or redefine the existing procurement process to make it environmentally friendly, the firm first needs to assess what products and services are most threatening to the environment. This involves applying the concept of an industrial ecosystem to the current production process; one which would facilitate the waste produced by one company to be used as resources by another. This type of industrial ecology would promote the sustainable use of renewable resource and minimal use of non-renewable ones. In order to achieve this stage, the organization would also naturally need managerial know-how to proportion the supply of green materials for production. The importance of generating public support for the proposed sustainable supply should not be underestimated. Indeed, informing the consumer is key in convincing them to change their habits and switch to responsible products while avoiding of course an image of "green washing."

An interesting innovation launched by Sodexo in Belgium offers a good example of how to successfully produce and launch responsible products and services. In 2010, the company introduced Eco-Pass cheques destined solely for the purchase of eco-citizen goods and services ranging from food or household items to the installation of solar panels or even eco-driving classes. Any purchase is valid as long as the item has respected an eco-citizen production process. This includes CO_2 emissions, recycling practices, etc. This innovation is particularly interesting as all impacts are taken into account from a macro and microeconomics perspective to the ecological and societal factors.

The process of development of responsible products and services consists of an integration of criteria linked to the project's impact on social, economic and environmental factors all along the innovation process, as illustrated in Figure 8.

In order to integrate responsibility all along the innovation process, the firm should set up a number of diagnostic tools to rate the new product or service in terms of its potential social, economic and environmental impacts. Naturally, not all impacts can be accurately measured during the pre-launch phase. These potential risks should be formulated into hypotheses to be tested once the product is on the market. In this way, an initial set of hypotheses should be created. These should be specified in the third stage of the process: "Capability," as the project itself becomes increasingly defined and new issues may be brought to light. In the "Post-Launch" phase, the hypotheses should be tested to clearly verify and measure the impacts of

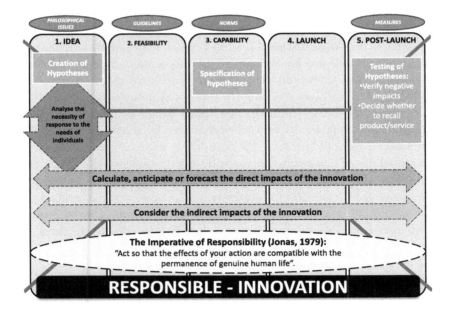

Figure 8.   A process for developing responsible products and services.
Source: Pavie and Carthy (2012).

the product or service and establish whether these are too great for the
latter to remain in circulation.

An analysis of the project's impact on various social, economic and
environmental factors should be integrated throughout the following five
steps:

Phase 1: Idea

The complexity involved with applying this technique in the idea phase
should not be under-estimated. Indeed, at this initial stage of the process,
it is crucial to let the innovator's imagination and ideas flow freely without
restriction. This is where the traditionally conflicting notions of responsibility and innovation may first enter into collision.

Within this first phase, relevant social factors to assess may include: the
degree of adaptability of the service or product to the disabled or the sick;
the possibility of access to the service for everybody regardless of age, sex
or religion — this factor would then need to be re-assessed following the
market launch to ensure it remains accessible to all; the extent to which

the new concept could contribute to social dialogue and communication on responsibility, while encouraging transparency — this criteria would once again require reviewing in the post-launch phase; the project's contribution to reducing exclusion and discrimination, and encouraging solidarity as well as freedom of access to fundamental rights for all; the impact on the diversity of habitats (eco-friendly constructions, "green" spaces, etc.) and its impact on wealth distribution and consumer health.

Secondly, the economic factors to be assessed could include the product's capability to encourage and foster responsible and ethical business activities — this would need to be thoroughly reviewed throughout the process and post-launch as it complies with the last stage of the model for achieving responsibility in an organization as mentioned previously (it becomes the responsible firm's duty to educate to responsibility); the extent to which the product or service facilitates a sustainable and inclusive economy including its potential effect on trade balance and employment rates as well as its impact on rural areas.

Thirdly, the environmental factors could determine the concept's impact on individuals' behavior in terms of the environment; its effect on the treatment of pollution and levels of nuisance with regard to the surrounding environment (air, water and soil pollution, movement and storage of dangerous products and wastes) and an estimate of the product's ecological footprint could also be calculated and reviewed post-launch.

In parallel to the measurement of the project's impacts in this initial phase a set of hypotheses relating to the impacts which may arise following the launch should be formulated. These will be specified later on in the process to be tested post-launch and will provide a more accurate indication of the project's impacts on social, economic and environmental factors.

Phase 2: Feasibility

Social factors to be tested in this second phase of the process could include the level of security for users, nearby residents and staff — this should be tested again in the following "Capability Phase"; the concept's impact on human resource development — this criteria would require a re-assessment following the launch; the impact on health, including the level of disease prevention, screening methods and treatment availability in the case of damage to health — this factor would need to be strictly reviewed following the launch to ensure the right procedures are put in place.

Economic factors required to be assessed could be the level of transparency towards the client in relation to any risks involved when using a product or service — this would need to be re-assessed following post-launch; security levels and confidentiality of data and transactions — this factor would need to be re-assessed following the launch of the product, along with its impact on competition levels and its reliability; the concept's influence on economic and territorial development, calculating the level of correlation between the service innovation and employment level and/or economic activity in the short and long-term.

Environmental factors to be examined would include ensuring that having taken all existing alternatives into account, the project guarantees the durability of energy resources; estimating its impact on behavior in terms of respecting the environment and the impact on environmental health (noise, pollution, water and air quality).

Phase 3: Capability

As the product or service being created becomes clearer in the "Capability phase," the firm should test social factors such as its impact on life and working conditions (the respect of the right of peaceful assembly and freedom of speech, working hours, security and hygiene) it should also re-examine previous factors such as the level of security for users, nearby residents and staff; the impact on health, with prevention, screening and treatment methods; the possibility of access to the service regardless of age, sex, religion, etc.; its adaptability for the disabled or the elderly and its impact on human resource management.

Economic factors to be re-assessed should include the level of security and confidentiality of data and transactions; the impact of the product or service on employment levels and its impact on land degradation. One factor in need of being newly assessed at this stage, would be the sub-contractors' willingness to conform to the firm's procedures regarding responsibility.

A number of environmental factors would also need to be re-assessed at this stage including the impact of the product or service on pollution and waste treatment, environmental health, landscape degradation as well as re-calculating the project's impact in terms of its ecological footprint.

The set of hypotheses should be specified in this stage of the process to ensure they remain relevant with the product/service being developed and will appropriately test the project for the correct impacts.

Phase 4: Launch

The number of factors which can be assessed at the "Launch Phase" is minimal as it is too early to re-calculate all measurable impacts. However, economic factors can be re-assessed, such as the level of correlation between the innovation and the employment level and/or economic activity in the short and long-term; transparency in terms of any risk to the consumer is crucial at this stage.

Social factors to be re-assessed include the contribution of the product or service to social dialogue and the encouragement of responsible communication and transparency.

Phase 5: Post-Launch

In this phase, the firm should ideally re-measure all previously estimated results and impacts, however budget constraints may not allow for such a costly procedure. In this case, it is essential for the firm to take into account the product or service being launched and the market it operates in to establish which factors require reviewing the most. For instance, factors which would typically need to be re-assessed for an online company include data security, which should be reviewed on a permanent basis to ensure optimum confidentiality and all data is kept securely. The impact of the new product or service on economic and territorial development, employment levels, as well as the degradation of rural areas should also be re-assessed. Social factors to be re-assessed include the innovation's impact on wealth distribution, its contribution to the fight against exclusion, discrimination, solidarity and access to fundamental rights for all. The firm should also ensure the product or service becomes part of its communication strategy surrounding responsibility and transparency.

The hypotheses which were formulated throughout the process should be tested at this stage. They should help the company monitor the impacts of its innovation once it is in circulation on the market.

In 2007, the Coca-Cola Recycling initiative was founded as part of the firm's CSR policy to support the Coca-Cola system's goal of recovering our footprint, recycling a bottle or can for every one we sell in North America. Coca-Cola Refreshments is a huge consumer and producer of PET plastic bottle and aluminium cans that are highly recyclable products. The initiative aims to incentivize consumers to recycle, provide with recycling points, set up a transformation industry, reuse recycled materials. In February 2009, Coca-Cola opened the world's largest PET bottle-to-bottle recycling plant which can produce PET plastic for reuse each year equivalent to 2 billion 20 ounce PET bottles. Grün line was founded by Adidas in 2008. Grün translates as green in German. Grün is a whole product line of eco-friendly shoes made of natural materials. Some shoes are specifically reshaped to give them an eco-allure, designed from scratch. But some are based on classic sneakers silhouettes, actually re-designed with new materials. There are three product lines "Made from" (original Adidas silhouettes made from environmentally friendly fibers in more colorful tones), "Recycled" (summery apparel and footwear made from recycled and reused materials), "Reground" (products made of environmentally friendly materials such as hemp, jute, bamboo, crepe rubber, chrome-free leather and recycled rice husks). Grün corresponds to an eco-apparel positioning, actually following entrepreneurial initiatives allying fashion and responsibility, like Veja or Fago projects.

e. Stage 5: *Lead the change*

This last stage of the process encourages the company to take a leadership role in its industry through three optional activities which are all ultimately linked to education. This may translate into campaigns aimed at educating customers on responsibility, creating an industry standard to educate other market players or developing new responsible business models to educate and raise awareness within the organization itself and among all employees.

i. *Communicate and educate to responsibility*

This optional stage of the model involves developing a planning tool to guide research dissemination regarding the characteristics of a responsible product. In order to fully integrate responsible innovation across the organization, the above steps do not suffice as they only concern the product positioning relative to competition. An organization's innovation activities are also responsible for improving the sense of responsibility patterns of production and consumption on the market as a whole. As a final stage, the firm needs to broadcast to the consumer and mobilize public attention to the topic of responsibility. Dissemination and implementation are complex processes, involving many disciplines and players within an organization. There is no one strategy or approach applicable to all situations. Researchers, therefore need to use multiple methods and tools to navigate their dissemination course.

An interesting example of a company communicating and educating customers to act responsibly is Sodexo. Sodexo encourages customers to make sustainable choices and adopt healthy, active lifestyles by developing several campaigns to spread awareness and information. Some of their initiatives are listed below:

- Student survival smartphone "app": In 2011, Sodexo launched a free smartphone "app," designed for students, which includes advice on how to lead a healthy lifestyle, cook balanced dishes, save energy and enhance their well-being.

- "Be part of it" menu range: Former England rugby star, Celebrity Master chef winner, and now Sodexo ambassador for health and well-being, Matt Dawson, launched the "Be part of it" menu range in May 2011. Its main objective is to raise awareness of health and well-being messages, encourage balanced diets and promote the use of fresh ingredients.
- Sustainability marques: In the spring of 2011, Sodexo launched a campaign across all our restaurants to explain our work around supply chain certification marques such as Fairtrade, the Marine Stewardship Council, RSPCA Freedom Foods, Red Tractor and LEAF (Linking Environment and Farming). The campaign included an information booklet for managers and large banners and posters to display in restaurants. It helped raise awareness of the marques, their meanings and their identifiable logos, giving customers the chance to better understand our offer and consider the marques when doing their own shopping.
- Healthy lifestyle booklet: As part of Healthworks offer, Sodexo provides customers with advice on balanced nutrition to match energy needs while exercising.
- Dedicated website: The website Healthwise provides nutrition and health education and coaching, including information on issues such as salt, fats, fluids and regular exercise.
- Nutritional information: Sodexo has developed a database of recipes with nutritional characteristics for each menu option. Their restaurants can now provide appropriate nutritional information depending on the audience, from calorie labeling to full GDA (Guideline Daily Amount) information.
- Nutrition game: They designed a board game called NVQ-qualified nutrition champions have designed a new board game to teach 5 to 11-year-old children about nutrition and healthy eating, which is available at primary schools served by Sodexo education.

McDonald's is another example of a company educating customers on responsibility. McDonald's has created a store following green building standards to lead by example and educate and encourage the customers in the matters of environmental sustainability. The store has an Energy Efficiency Education Dashboard in its premises which presents real-time energy efficiency data on the following:

- Various sustainable initiatives operating at the premises.

- It provides a link between the restaurant's solar photovoltaic array and the display board to provide real-time energy data in a user-friendly manner.
- The customers can interact with the 42-inch LCD touchscreen, to learn all about the sustainable features incorporated in the interior and exterior parts of the restaurant through a 3D tour.
- The customers are also encouraged to see a demonstration of how the solar photovoltaic system, LED lighting, solar hot water panels, Solar-tubes, porous pavers and other energy saving systems work.
- The aim is to educate and inspire people to implement green ideas in their personal lives.

Generali in its French market is also firmly involved in the communication and education of responsibility. Following the creation of its new "responsible generation" concept, the group highlight their four commitments in terms of responsibility[12]:

- Insure and invest — Protection of their clients and safeguard their interests;
- Mobilize and optimize — Manage their activities by focusing on human beings, optimize resources;
- Stimulate and anticipate — Encourage virtuous eco-friendly behavior to prepare the future; and
- Observe and reflect — Analyze the great evolutions of today's modern society.

Generali openly support a whole range of responsible initiatives, featured on their website, along with articles on various topics relating to responsibility including a clarification of the meaning of "green washing." In order to make it relevant and therefore catch the attention of the recipients, a wide range of topics are published from helping parents to choose responsible products for their children's back-to-school furniture to finding a "responsible" sporting activity (which even includes "Responsible Sport" charter to measure the responsibility of a particular activity).

ii. *Create standard*

This second optional stage of the process involves defining new norms and standards that address issues still "unknown" by providing new solutions. In

---

[12]Generali. Génération responsable: www.generation-responsable.com.

this case, the challenge facing the company is to source the required knowledge or expertise in terms of production impacts. While the organization needs to mobilize the attention of public authorities it should also aim to foster a genuine sense of interest, active reflection and involvement in current environmental, societal and economic impacts of its products and services.

In the same way that somebody once wondered whether it could become possible for humans to fly to the moon or dive deep down to explore the ocean floor, we must question the status quo now more than ever, aiming to address the societal grand challenges currently facing us (Nidumolu *et al.*, 2009).

A case in point is L'Oreal. L'Oreal has used scientific advances like tissue engineering, decoding the human genome, imaginary techniques to innovate responsibly. The use of the new generation testing methods makes it possible to evaluate the safety of ingredients without testing on animals. L'Oreal stopped testing finished products on animals in 1989 and in the near future will be able to evaluate clinical effectiveness without taking recourse to human tissue sampling. Its main objective is to stop *in vivo* animal testing and replace it with *in vitro* testing on the biological tissues that have been reconstructed in laboratories. L'Oreal's Gerland Center produces 11 models of different biological tissue (epidermis, dermis, cornea, etc.). Reconstructed skin replaces animal testing in 99% of studies.

iii.   *Develop responsible business models*

With this type of innovation, the firm aims to find new ways to provide and capture value, which will form a new basis for competition. In order to do this, the firm must focus on understanding customer needs and identify ways to meet these needs as well as understand how business partners are able to add value to the offering. Three focus areas need to be looked at by Chief Information Officers when expanding and facilitating business model innovation efforts:

a. Deepen business understanding through componentization;
b. Innovate the IT business model first; and
c. Implement a flexible, responsive infrastructure.

The value chain needs to be looked at as a whole, with the aim of involving both suppliers and customers simply interacting with a different form of consumption. In 2008, FedEx implemented the innovative organizational program "Fuel Sense" designed to replace its fleet with Boeing 757, thus reducing jet fuel consumption by nearly 36%, while increasing capacity by 20%. They further developed software to optimize flight routes and in certain cases to use solar energy for its centers based in California and Germany.

One can take a look at IBM's Business model innovation discussed in IBM's Global CEO Study 2006. The report reveals that CEOs are expanding the innovation horizon to gain a more expansive and unconventional view of innovation. While CEOs still believe that product, service and operational innovations are important, they feel that innovation must also be applied to a company's very core — to the way it does business and drives revenue. Technology is universally viewed as a driving force and enabler for innovation. The role of IT and of the CIO in driving business model innovation has never been more important. In the Global CEO Study, CEOs identified "inflexible physical and IT infrastructure" and 'insufficient access to information" as two of the top 10 obstacles to innovation. To add value to businesses and support innovation, IT organizations need to rethink their role in the business environment. CIOs who are looking to expand and facilitate their companies' business model innovation efforts should take action in three focus areas:

1. Deepen business understanding through componentization: Componentization enables IT organizations to understand the business processes that drive revenue for the organization, and this allows them to prioritize IT investments for the greatest gains.
2. Innovate the IT business model first: By seeing IT as a business rather than a cost-center and identifying the IT processes that add the most value, company leaders can make investments, shift personnel and reallocate resources where they will have the greatest impact. IT can then respond quickly to the ever-changing business needs.
3. Implement a flexible, responsive infrastructure: The first step in creating a more agile infrastructure is the consolidation and simplification of existing technologies. CIOs have to leverage open standards and infrastructure technologies like virtualization and autonomic computing, which are designed to accommodate unpredictable change, improve efficiency and reduce the time to market for new business capabilities.

The efficient integration of responsibility evidently contributes to a positive image,[13] making the organization increasingly appealing to various

---

[13]Dubigeon, O (2009). *Piloter un développement responsable. Quels processus pour l'entreprise?* 3e Edition. Paris: Pearson Village Mondial.

stakeholder groups and strengthening its viability. In the meantime, the responsible innovation process guarantees its sustainable competitiveness and performance needed to survive.

An attractive brand image

A responsible organization contributes positively to its reputation through the last step of the process involving communication to the ecosystem, educating stakeholders in relation to its responsible processes and actions undertaken by the firm. The differentiation advantage developed through this method enhances the firm's brand image as it openly demonstrates its ability to react and adapt to societies' ever evolving demands and expectations. There are now instruments specifically aimed at assessing a firm's level of responsibility in order to, on the one hand, reward those which are actively pursuing responsible practices and encourage them as well as others to manage their business in a similar way. These reward methods contribute to further impact positively on the corporate image, whether it is from an economic point of view through positive discrimination taxes and administrative authorization for instance, or from a perspective of ratings, indexing, specific rewards and media communication. Conversely, instruments aimed at denouncing firms which engage in dishonest practices provide a means for penalizing certain structures which might be involved in "green-washing" among others. The increasing influence of social media networks in the consumer's decision-making process has aggravated the catastrophic consequences for the firm which receives such an "anti-reward".

Retaining investors has always been of critical importance for the organization's survival, but the volatility of the former has widely increased, as they need to keep up with market trends. The financial community's ease of access to the responsible organization's capital fund information and the stakeholders' accessibility to its process for integrating responsibility helps to build loyalty among these critical actors by reassuring them on the transparency of the company as a whole.

The ecosystem-based restructuring of the value chain fosters the development of durable relationships with suppliers, as the organization favors proximity, loyalty and collaborative intelligence. By selecting those which are actively engaged in integrating responsibility across their organization and processes — which increasingly secures suppliers and stakeholders — the access to resources is guaranteed, while the cost and quality of raw materials are optimized.

From an employee's point of view, it is generally preferable to work in a responsible company. Indeed, the raised awareness triggered by recent market events has led an increasing number of high-potential students to look for future employment at firms which are seriously and actively involved in responsible activities. The latter strengthens an sense of pride and belonging among employees, who are in turn self-motivated, leading to an improved level of productivity, quality and reliability across the organization.

A source of strengthened viability

The second phase of the process which involves anticipating future legal requirements means that the responsible organization is constantly aiming at staying ahead of competition and market trends by adapting itself early to suit future potential legislation changes, which are increasingly demanding in terms of public and private procurement processes. The credibility which the firm acquires through its responsibility integration process renders it increasingly influential and involved in working groups responsible for developing current laws.[14]

In order to keep developing, the responsible organization requires an efficient and sustainable type of governance. The latter needs to be based on collaborative intelligence and is therefore capable of directly addressing any upcoming issues raised by stakeholders.[15]

The process for integrating responsibility includes a proactive method of management for risks and opportunities linked to various social, economic and environmental factors. This is done through the creation of hypotheses, which forms an integral part of the responsible innovation process.

This process is advantageous in the case of insurance, as agencies will provide covers more readily to firms which follow a specific process for integrating responsibility, thereby actively representing a lower level of risk.

In the same way, financial institutions will generally trust structures which are less likely to end up in court over their actions or generate extra costs linked to negative impacts which could have been better anticipated.

---

[14]Dubigeon, O (2009). *Piloter un développement responsable. Quels processus pour l'entreprise?* 3e Edition. Paris: Pearson Village Mondial.
[15]*Ibid.*

By carefully achieving a balance which fosters a global stability and by monitoring the impacts which its new products and services may have on social, economic and environmental factors, the responsible business contributes to the consolidation of markets through the elimination of dishonest and corrupt practices. This also contributes to the preservation of both the local and global environment by integrating a process for managing negative impacts at the heart of the innovation process. Societal balance therefore becomes regulated through the monitoring of impacts. Some of these are direct threats to human and environmental health, which in turn affect working conditions and employability and eventually impact on the conditions of the company's viability in the long term.

This five-stage model illustrated in Figure 9 aims to serve as a guide for organizations wishing to implement responsible innovation across their activities. Indeed, in order to position a firm as innovative and responsible a course of defined actions must be strictly followed to ensure responsibility is implemented at all levels. Following these stages rigorously ensures that the corporate image does not get tainted by "green washing," while guaranteeing that the firm's responsible innovation strategy remains centered on generating innovation, growth and performance.

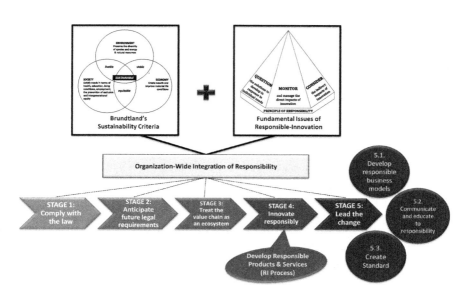

Figure 9.   A process for integrating responsible innovation.[15]

3. An Evaluation of Responsible Innovation

Following Brundtland's pillars, one could argue whether responsibility is reached if one or more of the sustainable development pillars are increased in value, to the expense or not of another pillar. Since it is difficult to accurately define the parameter of responsibility with regards to innovation, we suggest a method for assessing a responsible innovation in terms of its degree of responsibility. The extent to which an organization has engaged in responsible innovation can be broken down into separate levels, ranging from very little or almost no responsibility (throughout the innovation process and after launch) to higher levels of responsibility. In the case of the latter, social, economic and environmental factors have all proactively been taken into account in the light of the three axes of responsible innovation.

The first level is that of very little or almost no responsible innovation where existing products are added with small improvements (e.g. services, processes, organizations, business models, management practices). These improvements do not significantly change the way the product solve problems or the way in which they are used. The characteristic of the nil-level responsible innovation is, for example, that it provides economic value at the expense of social or environmental value.

The second level is about moderate responsible innovation. Here one of the values is increased without compromising the other two. It can be written as following:

- Social value increases while economic and environmental value remain equal;
- Environmental value increases while economic and social value remain equal; and
- Economic value increases while social and environmental value, remain equal.
- In the latter some might argue that it has little to do with sustainability, however, if economic welfare increases social welfare and solves poverty, it follows the values of Brundtland's pillars.

The third level is about **positive responsible innovation**, where two or more values are increased. A clear example here is that of security cameras in public spaces, the interplay between privacy versus security, see

---

[15]Pavie, X and Carthy, D (2013). *Op. cit.*

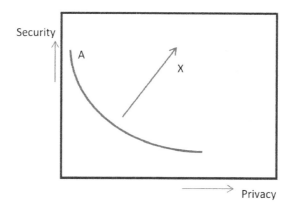

Figure 10.   Interplay between security and privacy.

Figure 10. Similar interrelations can also be found in sustainability versus economy, etc.

Line A is such that if security increases the level of privacy is decreasing, while if we try to have higher levels of privacy, the security goes down. In such a case, the innovator is struggling with the problem that he may increase the level of security at the expense of privacy, or vice versa, he can increase the privacy of people but it will be detrimental for the security. This poses the problem of moral overload to the innovator.[16] Overcoming the problem of moral overload requires to innovate in the direction of arrow X. For instance smart security cameras that activate only when certain criteria are violated such as a specific sound or strange behavior might be solution to maintain security and privacy both at high levels. These types of innovations can be considered responsible innovations at the product dimension, and the problem of moral overload becomes a source for responsible innovation where technology is providing the opportunity to solve the problem. In general we would argue that the third level of responsible innovation is reached if:

- Increase of *economic* and *social* value with *environmental* value remaining equal;
- Increase of *economic* and *environmental* value with *social* value remaining equal;

---

[16]Van den Hoven, MJ, Lokhorst, G and van de Poel, I (2012). Engineering and the problem of moral overload. *Science and Engineering Ethics*, 18, 1–13.

- Increase of *social* and *environmental* value with *economic* value remaining equal; and
- Increase of all values simultaneously.

Balancing the social, economic and environmental values is highly multifaceted, inherently global and grand in scope and scale. As previously mentioned, the issues linked to responsible innovation share the same characteristics as wicked problems. Indeed, as innovation and the business environment are by nature uncertain, it is highly difficult to predict the potential success as well as impacts surrounding the launch of a new product or service. We examined earlier the consequences of this uncertainty for the innovator. In the case of the policy-maker, it is generally insufficient to attempt addressing a problem or issue through a single policy, or rational approach. These are far more complex situations, whereby a new policy addressing one aspect of a problem may uncover new issues which were previously completely unknown.

Interesting conceptual discussions are for instance the case where one of the values is decreased while the other values are increased and the total of the three new values is more than before, in other words:

$$(\mathbf{V}\text{Econ.}_{t=1} + \mathbf{V}\text{Social}_{t=1} + \mathbf{V}\text{Environment}_{t=1})$$
$$> (\mathbf{V}\text{Econ.}_{t=0} + \mathbf{V}\text{Social}_{t=0} + \mathbf{V}\text{Environment}_{t=0})$$

where,

$$\text{Value-Econ.}_{t=1} < \text{Value} - \text{Econ.}_{t=0;} \text{ or}$$
$$\text{Value-Social}_{t=1} < \text{Value} - \text{Social}_{t=0;} \text{ or}$$
$$\text{Value-Environment}_{t=1} < \text{Value} - \text{Environment}_{t=0.}$$

a. *Responsible innovation: A product and process dimension*

In defining an issue as complex as RI it is useful to return to basic terminology. Central is the concept of innovation as some form of novelty that leads to value creation within the market. Similarly, if we continue the discussion on responsibility we can conclude that responsibility is aimed at balancing the triple bottom line of economic, social and environmental value. However, since innovation is a process and comes with management practices, various discussions have emerged and argue that responsible innovation has a product dimensions which is reflected in the outcome of the innovation process

Table 6.   Product and process dimensions of responsible innovation.[17]

Product dimension	Process dimension
Market and economically viable	Deployment of codes Accountability: standards, certification, accreditation
Ethically acceptable	
Sustainable	Ethics as a design factor
Socially desirable	Innovation is not seen as an aim in itself but a contributing factor to the overall good.
Environmental	
	Moral responsibility and legal responsibility

and a process dimension, which is about the posture and philosophy one has when conducting the innovation process, see Table 6.[18]

The *product dimension* deals with the outcome of the innovation itself. This product can be either a feasible product or a service or a new business model, see the dimensions of innovation. Various scholars have attached requirements that innovations should meet before they can be considered responsible. First, the requirement is as in the definition of innovation that it should be market ready and economically feasible to bring the product to the market. But in addition to that, the innovation should be ethically acceptable, it should be environmentally sustainable and socially desirable. These requirements follow the values along the three pillars of Brundtland.

The *process dimension* is addressing the governance of innovation. While conducting the activities in the innovation process, the process can be considered responsible if it includes the deployment of certain codes, standards, certification and accreditation, if the eventual contribution of the innovation is aimed at the overall good including ethical issues and holds moral and legal responsibility. In this dimension, the responsible innovation is associated with various conceptual aspects of responsibility, such as moral, legal and role responsibility which are principle concerns of ethics. In order to make these conceptualizations more tangible, various researchers

---

[17]Von Schomberg, R (2013). A vision of responsible innovation. In Owen, R, Heintz, M and Bessant, J (Eds.), *Responsible Innovation*. London: John Wiley, forthcoming.

[18]*Ibid.*

have addressed management practices to the innovation process and if these are included, the innovation process is considered to be more responsible and so its outcome will be according the Brundtland framework.

The management practices should include elements of anticipatory, inclusive, responsive and reflective.[19] Stakeholder engagement is one management practice to be inclusive and anticipatory. It is a process by which an organization involves people who may be affected by the decisions it makes during the innovation process. These people can support or oppose the decisions, be influential in the organization or within the community in which the company operates. As a result they may affect the success of an innovation in the long term. The importance of engaging stakeholders is crucial, particularly when solving multiple dilemmas.

A solution to increase the value of one pillar might have consequences, which are difficult to foresee, in another pillar of the Brundtland framework. This is mainly due to the bounded rationality of individuals.[20] The argument is that individuals are only partly rational in the decisions they make and in most of their decisions they are emotional and even irrational. Individuals have limitations to formulating the problem, solve complex models and processing (receiving, storing, retrieving, transforming) information. Individuals tend to follow heuristics when searching for a solution. The heuristics is that they tend to rely on experience-based techniques for problem solving, learning, and discovery. Following a more rigorous and rational approach to solve the problem in order to find the optimal solution requires the inclusion of various viewpoints and the analysis and comparison of all possible solutions. However, individuals are limited in their time and financial resources which puts pressure on their ability to process and compute the expected utility of every alternative action, in particular in more complex situations. As a result individuals are bounded rational and look for satisfying answers, which means that they deliberate only long enough to come up with good enough course of actions. In various literatures, this is discussed as neighborhood or local search among the solutions close to the experience and capabilities an organization has. Incremental search is also related to this, because by taking small steps the actions and consequences can be overseen and one can adapt to the new knowledge.

---

[19] Owen, R, Macnaghten, P and Stilgoe, J (2012). Responsible research and innovation: From science in society to science for society, with society. *Science and Public Policy*, 39(6), 751–760.

[20] Simon, HA (1957). *Models of Man*. New York: Wiley & Sons.

The inclusion of stakeholders can prevent the company from following a certain path to find a solution to a problem which may bring out other problems once introduced in the market. A flexible approach to the innovation process is required to change its path of search for a solution once stakeholders inform on potential problems in the future. Various methodologies have been developed to help the company in this respect. Technology Assessment (TA) is often used to identify the effect certain new technologies have on society. The main premise is that new technological developments affect the world at large rather than just the customers being targeted, and as a result technological progress can never be free of ethical implications. Although traditional TA is at the level of society and tries to identify the repercussions on society of a specific technology, recent advancements such as Constructive Technology Assessment (CTA) attempts to broaden the design of new technology by including feedback of TA activities into the actual construction of technology. Contrary to other forms of TA, CTA is not directed toward influencing regulatory practices by assessing the impacts of technology. Instead, CTA wants to address social issues around technology by influencing design practices.[21] Also, foresight studies and future studies are methods to forecast the kinds of futures that will be the result of new technologies and which technologies are needed in future. They help building the scenarios, an early warning system (EWS), to determine which scenario is (or will be) the dominant one and in which direction society might be moving.[22]

Solving the society's grand challenges and escaping moral dilemmas requires an approach which is associated with thinking-outside the box and including stakeholders to signal the repercussions of an innovation in terms of social, ethical and environmentally desirable for various people early on during the innovation process. Similarly it is important to remain flexible throughout the innovation process in order to change the direction by which the company tries to find a solution. Future studies and constructive technology assessment which act as early warning systems can help companies to be responsive and anticipatory during its innovation process and reflect on the technologies and applications they are about to bring to the

---

[21]Schot, J and Rip, A (1997). The past and future of constructive technology assessment. *Technological Forecasting & Social Change*, 54, 251–268.
[22]Botterhuis, L, van der Duin, P, de Ruijter, P and van Wijck, P (2010). Monitoring the future. Building an early warning system for the Dutch Ministry of Justice. *Futures*, 42, 454–465.

market. In this way, innovation management is *inclusive* in terms of considering relevant stakeholders, *anticipatory* that it holds an eye watching on technical and societal developments and *responsive* to change its direction of technology and product development. Consequently we can consider that the company adopts a responsible posture towards its innovation process.

b. *Success of responsible innovation*

Success of responsible innovation can be discussed in various ways. The first condition flows from the general notion of innovation success. Thus, a successful responsible innovation is first and foremost characterized by a successful market introduction, leading to the creation of value for the organization. Indeed, the main objective of a responsible innovation is to be economically sustainable and to contribute positively to organizational performance, while integrating in parallel the three axes of responsible-innovation all along the innovation process. This should take place within an organization aiming to be responsible, through the five-stage process introduced earlier. A responsible innovation needs to ultimately add value, once the organization has considered whether or not to answer to a particular consumer need and is actively monitoring direct and indirect impacts related to the new product or service. It becomes clear at this stage that the success of a responsible innovation — whose final objective neither needs to be specifically social nor environmental, but rather consists in providing added value while taking potential impacts into consideration — cannot be measured in terms of providing a set positive or negative answer. Rather, the implementation of a responsible innovation strategy and process ensures that the organization's performance objectives are fully accounted for through the innovation process, while impacts are monitored and needed alterations are actively worked on in order to minimize or eliminate the negative impacts on the society and ecosystem. The success of a responsible innovation may therefore be measured in terms of its degree of responsibility, once it has followed the required development process and attracted enough customers to be profitable.

For instance, the General Motors' (GM) EV-1, the world's first mass-produced and purpose-designed electric vehicle, was taken from the market despite positive customer reaction to it. According to GM, electric cars occupied an unprofitable niche of the automobile market, and the manufacturer decided to take in return all automobiles and crush them regardless of protesting customers. Had the EV-1 been profitable for GM, it could have been believed that the EV-1 would be a successful responsible innovation, in terms of providing social and economic value from the customers' perspective. However, since the EV-1's first objective was to provide a means of transport which aimed specifically at reducing its environmental impact, the question should concern the impact of its production process. In this case, the latter is subject to controversial debate due to the extraction and use of rare earth minerals. Indeed, the launch of such 'green' products, whose development process does not seem to be taken into account with regards to its impact often results in green-washing. The critical importance of taking the impacts of the innovation and production process into consideration is also highlighted in the debate of heavy fuel consuming cars, such as the mass-produced Hummer and the Toyota Prius. Researchers from CNW Marketing[23] have shown that, based on life cycle analysis, the energy use over their entire life cycles from raw materials extraction and manufacturing, to driving and burning fuel, to the recycling and disposal of parts, the Hummer performs in environmental terms much better than the Prius. Although the study is claimed controversial[24] it sheds light on the difficulty to provide clear cut indicators of success of responsible innovation.

However, these examples reveal that the condition of successful market introduction which applies to innovation in general is not enough to label an innovation as responsible. The performance of responsible innovation lies in contributing to the values of the Triple Bottom Line of Brundtland: economic, social and environmental. In a recent research in Denmark, Kramer, Pfitzer and Lee[25] found that with regards to Corporate Social Responsibility in general, many companies still cannot measure or track the costs and benefits — or the competitive value — associated with their CSR activities. The main concern lies in the fact that these activities lacked the measurable economic rationale to indicate the benefits CSR initiatives. However,

---

[23] CNW Marketing Research Inc. (2007). Dust to Dust: The Energy Cost of New Vehicles From Concept to Disposal.

[24] Gleick, PH (2007). Hummer versus Prius. "Dust to Dust" report Misleads the Media and Public with Bad Science. *CNW Marketing*.

[25] Kramer, M, Pfitzer, M and Lee, P (2005). Competitive social responsibility: Uncovering the economic rationale for corporate social responsibility among Danish small- and medium-sized enterprises. Foundation Strategy Group & Center for Business and Government, John F. Kennedy School of Government, Harvard University. [Online]. Available: http://www.eogs.dk/sw26505.asp. Accessed on 20 August 2009.

indicators of employee retention, job performance, use of raw materials and energy use are considered to be all direct and inherent components of SME cost structures and if CSR practices affect these, they can be linked directly to competitiveness and productivity. Similarly for responsible innovation the effect of the innovation outcome, the product or service, can be measured in terms of impact on each of the three pillars, however, it remains difficult to make statements in terms of success regarding the time dimension (prospective versus retrospective). If we consider the case of products composed of asbestos, we can see the clear need for the creation of hypotheses by the company engaging in responsible innovation. At the time it was launched, innovators could not have foreseen the exact impacts its product would have, in fact it was initially praised for its sound absorption, its resistance to fire, heat, electrical and chemical damage, and cost-efficiency, which made it compatible with Brundtland's three dimensions. However, when the toxicity of the mineral was uncovered, manufacturers had not been prepared for such a scenario, which had disastrous consequences. If organizations which were using asbestos as part of their production processes had put in place a set of hypothesis to test for toxicity of minerals used, it could have better prepared for the damage that followed.[26] This example shows that the creation of hypotheses can assist companies in dealing with the temporal characteristic of innovation.

c. *Key challenges associated with responsible innovation*

The success of responsible innovation is to some extent subject to the temporal perceptions people have about the repercussions an innovation has regarding the social, economic and environmental values of the Brundtland framework. This, therefore, may vary throughout the innovation development process, once the innovation is launched, as well as long after its introduction.

The innovation funnel is a picture that illustrates how innovation goals, innovation actions, innovation teams and innovation results interact with each other and change over time. In essence, the funnel begins (t = 0) with various ideas and thoughts where many decisions have to be made. Here the main discipline is sketching and at later stages to the end of the

---

[26] Alleman, JE and Brooke, TM (1997). Asbestos revisited. *Scientific American*, July, 70–75.

funnel, a more refined design can be tested by building prototypes to test the usability of the ideas which was decided upon in earlier stages. The further we get into the world of prototyping, the more time and resources we have invested in the process, and the more focused our design becomes; this is represented by the funnel in our illustration. Thus, as the decisions are made and time progresses the purpose and the characteristics of an innovation become clearer. The innovation follows a certain path and with every decision made, the degrees of freedom generally diminish. The funnel also shows that there is a significant time lag between the invention and the eventual application of that invention in products and services, referring to the Collingridge dilemma as previously mentioned.

4. From the Precautionary Principle to a Responsible Innovation Code?

Should we launch an innovation when we do not know exactly all the impacts which can ensue? Should a type of Precautionary Principle be specifically developed to suit the economic environment, in a context where competitive market pressure is precisely the sole reason for innovation to generate a competitive advantage?

Let us first remind ourselves of what the Precautionary Principle entails. A relatively new principle, intimately linked to scientific development, it was first recognized at the United Nations Conference on Environment and Development (UNCED) which took place in 1992 in Rio de Janeiro, Brazil. While science exercised its power during its reign of knowledge and incontestability until the end of the 20th century, it is now becoming increasingly uncertain and subject to debates and controversies. As a result, political, health and governmental authorities are often faced with issues and risks whose consequences are completely unknown. This Precautionary Principle concerns above all risks for the environment and human health. If these risks are not clearly proven, they must be nonetheless argued in the most scientific way possible. If limitations remain in the latter case, then public authorities must bear responsibility for the risks incurred based on the stated objectives.

This principle was introduced into the French Constitution in 2004 as part of the Charter for the Environment. Thus, Article 5 states: "when the occurrence of damage, even uncertain in light of the existing and available scientific knowledge, could seriously affect and have irreversible consequences on the environment, public authorities shall ensure the application of the Precautionary Principle and the deployment of specific procedures for evaluating risks as well as the adoption of temporary and proportionate measures to prepare for any eventuality within their particular field of activity. It is important to note that the Precautionary Principle applies to a potential risk whose probability and consequences are immeasurable. This differentiates it from the Principle of Prevention which applies to an identified risk, whose probability and consequences are therefore proven and evaluated.

The Precautionary Principle should not be understood as an obstacle to innovation. On the contrary, it means increasing scientific studies and research, evaluating the levels of risks with regards to uncertainties in order to increase knowledge in a specific field and hence better identify and understand potential dangers. No scientific development should be restricted on the grounds of the Precautionary Principle since scientific research is in fact the very means which can lead to a breakthrough in terms of evaluating risks. Thus, applying the Precautionary Principle to nanotechnologies, for instance, essentially means increasing research, tests and studies to achieve a common knowledge that is both shared and as reliable as possible.

While Jonas recommends restraint in terms of launching new technological projects if the information regarding its safety is considered insufficient, he does not suggest that such restraint should be permanent. Indeed, Eric Pommier (2012) also indicates that our responsibility does not consist in interrupting research, since developing that very activity will help us make progress in terms of anticipating risks more efficiently, measuring negative impacts more accurately and gaining more accurate knowledge of critical levels among other factors.[27] In fact, technical research should be encouraged for two main reasons, according to Jonas; namely for the benefits it provides and also because it contributes to finding the countermeasures needed for addressing the upcoming challenges we are facing in terms of the society, environment and economy. It is therefore, a question of making that progress, responsibly.

The Precautionary Principle can also be used to ban a certain technology if it seems harmful to society. There is no question of *The* Precautionary Principle but rather *A* Precautionary Principle which is used and applied in differing ways depending on the various stages an innovation is at. It

---

[27]Pommier, E (2012). *Hans Jonas et le Principe Responsabilité*. Paris: Presses Universitaires de France.

therefore aims at either taking precautionary measures with regards to the uncertain nature of risks or at delaying the deployment of certain projects as long as the risks have not been clearly identified.

The Precautionary Principle shares this characteristic of uncertainty with responsible innovation: the damage has not been caused and is not even certain of happening. This also differentiates it from curative action, whose aim is to repair. The main difference between the Precautionary Principle and responsible innovation is the fact that in the first case, the action is restrained. In other words, applying the Precautionary Principle by not launching the innovation, engenders risks, which this time have little to do with the environment or human health but are rather related to the organization's competitiveness.

What should therefore become of a potential innovation project which would provide a competitive advantage, but which is not fully under control in terms of responsibility? A preferable option would be to develop a *Principle of Care*[28] with the aim of "minding," "taking care of," and ensuring the welfare of fellow human beings. This principle would therefore not limit innovation, but rather provide a monitoring framework throughout the development of the project all the way to the market launch. Scientists do not have the answer to every question, every doubt; neither do innovators. Investigations do not always lead to conclusive evidence regarding possible consequences of a project which has not yet been launched. Furthermore, scientific and marketing analyses are generally conducted in laboratories or in market tests, which does not accurately represent the reality of consumer behavior.

The decision to launch or not a particular innovation would therefore become dependent on the identification of an acceptable level of risk linked to the project, given the knowledge available at the time of market launch.

In parallel, this monitoring system also entails the need to speculate with regards to risks and potential consequences and make a number of assertions along the following lines:

- Risk evaluation: What are the propensities to exceed targets and the risks of failure?
- Risk management: From the moment an assumption starts revealing negative impacts, how do we react? What frameworks, procedures must be put in place to allow for this type of management?

---

[28]Pavie, X (2011). The importance of responsible innovation and the necessity of innovation-care. *Working Paper ESSEC 1203.*

- Communication: How can we communicate, both internally and potentially externally, on the risks that we are aware we are taking and that are being fully controlled by applying the preventive measures put in place within our organization?

The Principle of Care — or *Responsible Innovation Code* — would seem better suited than the Principle of Precaution to the specificities of a competitive economic context, where innovation needs to be fostered. No executive director will stop an innovation if the level of risk is low — his own pressure from economic and performance factors will push him forward in terms of deciding to launch a new project onto the market. Hence, practices must be supervised, not discouraged, potential consequences should be anticipated, explained instead of imposing sanctions. Sanctions and prohibitions cause the diversion into another space, another time. In an innovation context, the Principle of Care would not address the question of whether or not to act but would rather tackle the issue: We will act, how do we do it?

While kindness and care for others are key notions in the context of innovation-care, it is important to note at this stage that the word care is nevertheless subordinate to the idea of innovation. Despite the fact that an innovator-carer should have the ability to decide when to give up on an innovation, their first objective is to achieve economic performance in their activity. Rather than being a frame or a brake to innovation, care should rather be a process articulated to and with it. It is not the final goal of innovation, since the latter is measured and evaluated in terms of performance, growth, sustainability of the organization and improvement of the individual's life.[29]

This also helps understanding from an international perspective.[30] While the Precautionary Principle is particularly heterogeneous, the Principle of Care or Responsible Innovation Code is, by definition, applicable internationally, since it involves "doing," but according to certain conditions. As such, the Responsible Innovation Code would be an ideal tool for innovation, particularly suited to its specificities, while the Precautionary Principle can rather be seen as an obstacle in that context.[31]

Jonas believes that the freedom of research can no longer be without limits. Research should continue, as it will potentially provide solutions for

---

[29]Pavie, X (2012). The importance of responsible-innovation and the necessity of innovation-care. *Op. cit.*

[30]De Sadeleer, N (2011). *Le Principe de précaution dans le monde.* Paris: Fondapol.

[31]Pavie, X (2012). *Innovation-responsable: Stratégie et levier de croissance des organisations. Op. cit.*

solving the grand challenges of society, however, it must be supported and monitored by ethical principles. He explores the possibility of creating a sort of National Order for Researchers which, if we were to imagine in a similar way a National Order for Innovators, would be responsible for involving members from civil society (all of whom are directly or indirectly impacted by these projects) to establish whether or not a particular project should be launched. However, such a structure would eventually become once again dependent on achieving short-term interests.

An alternative option could be to raise the researcher or in our case the innovator's awareness with regards to the impact of their own work on society. The philosopher's first responsibility, which is also that of the researcher and therefore the innovator's, is lucidity. This lucidity is the absolute prerequisite to the creation of an ethics committee.[32] Those who are most likely to know which types of innovation require to be tested are also those who are most likely to be impacted by the test outcomes. Those who are the least informed are also generally those who have the least personal interest and involvement and are therefore more suitable to make the decision. It is therefore, a question of finding a balance of powers between the informed opinion of innovators whose personal interests are directly at stake and the objectivity and lack of knowledge of members of society.[33]

Innovation processes are made up of a complex set of various dynamics, differing actors and partners. They are the ultimate combination of various disciplines, all driven towards achieving the same strategic vision driving initiated by their leader. The complexities associated with this process are both internal and external. From an internal perspective, the innovation value chain from the strategic objective to the management of human resources is very intricate. Many of these dimensions are supported by an external ecosystem made up of both partners (suppliers, universities, centers of expertise and competitiveness, etc.) and consumers (who have their say on current issues). The aim of this scheme is to understand all porosities between innovation structures and citizens, in other words how the latter are affected by innovations. For that reason, we introduce the idea of motives for responsible innovation. These motives (whether they be partners, markets, customer needs and innovation structures) are those that bear the responsibility for the innovation; a responsible innovation Code must therefore acquire a meaning and an existence around these very

---

[32] Jonas, H (1979). *Op. cit.*
[33] *Ibid.*

dimensions. It is within the latter that the questions discussed previously must be addressed: Should we always answer consumer needs? Are we able to measure the impacts of our innovation on customers? Are we also able to measure the indirect impacts of that same innovation on citizens? Organizations are subject to various issues, porosities, strategies which are put into place throughout the process, while they also stand under increasing pressure from the surrounding environment. For that reason, a responsible innovation code should be shared by all, citizens and organizations, partners and consumers, for the common good of all (Figure 11).[34]

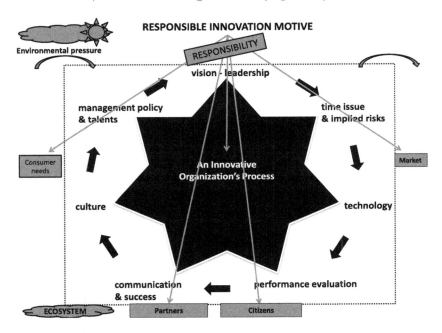

Figure 11. Actors affected by the responsible innovation code.[35]

---

[34]Pavie, X (2012). *Innovation-responsable: Stratégie et levier de croissance des organisations. Op. cit.*
[35]Pavie, X (2012). *Innovation-responsable: Stratégie et levier de croissance des organisations. Op. cit.*

4
POLICY CASE FOR RESPONSIBLE INNOVATION

As innovation policy covers a wide range of objectives, both economic (productivity growth, employment and competitiveness) and non-economic ones (cultural, social, environmental and military), governments often intervene in the innovation process to ensure that public policy objectives will be achieved. Before a government intervenes there needs to be a clear rationale for the intervention and an understanding that the intervention will resolve the issue. To date, the primary reason why governments intervene in the economy is market failure. Market failures can occur due to the existence of externalities, spill-overs, imperfect and asymmetric information, network failures and market power. In terms of responsible innovation, one of the most pressing market failures is the existence of externalities, both positive and negative. These externalities are effects of production and consumption that are not properly reflected in market signals. In terms of responsible innovation, a negative externality can be the costs for mitigating pollution that are not incurred by the polluter or reflected in the price of the product in the market. A positive externality can be through the public good benefits of an innovation, e.g. flu vaccinations. System failures are linked to structural, institutional and regulatory deficiencies, which effect innovation activities. The system failures argument justifies interventions that address structural and institutional deficiencies. Although they can be seen as complementary, economists differentiate between market failures and system failures. The systems perspectives emphasize the importance of interaction and interactive learning among all actors in the system. In the case of systems failure, the processes of intervention are similar in the case of market failure although the process is not focused on recreating market conditions or optimum economic efficiency. Some of the key characteristics of systems failure interventions include increased collaboration and interactivity, a focus on learning and tacit knowledge, innovation capacity building, flexible and responsive policy frameworks and increased policy coherence.

It is important to note that both market failures and system failures are arguments used to justify policy intervention. In the forthcoming Framework Program "Horizon 2020," the European Commission will make responsible innovation a key topic. The vision of Horizon 2020 is to achieve "smart, sustainable and inclusive growth" within the European Union. Aside from the regulatory and adaptive governance role, policy will play a key role in raising awareness of the large number of responsible innovation opportunities and create the necessary incentives to upscale current and future markets. In the coming years, the association between regulation and responsible innovation will be strong and positive. Although companies facing stringent regulation will most likely become engaged in responsible innovation, and we would like to address the role policy that can stimulate companies to become more entrepreneurial and identify the opportunities related to responsible innovation. In particular, we are interested in the behavioral additionalities of policy instruments. Behavioral additionality has received recent discussion as a benefit of investments for start-ups besides the traditional input and output benefits of financial support. The concept of behavioral additionality is discussed by Falk[1] who argues that public support contributes to firms by increasing their scope to acquire new knowledge. In general, managers are bounded by the high-pressure of daily activities[2] and disregard the value of new knowledge, unless it emerges from areas where the firm is currently carrying out activities and funding. Public support may bring out behavioral additionalities in terms of changes in the mind-set of people, posture of firms and changes in the firm's innovation processes.

With regards to the grand challenges of today's society, it seems that we need new emerging technologies which can solve problems for which we have

---

[1]Falk, R (2007). Measuring the effects of public support schemes on firms' innovation activities. Survey evidence from Austria. *Research Policy*, 36(5), 665–679.
[2]Fransman, M (1990). *The Market and Beyond: Cooperation and Competition in Information Technology Development in the Japanese System*. Cambridge: Cambridge University Press. Georghiou, L *et al.* (2003). Raising EU R&D intensity: Improving the effectiveness of public support mechanisms for private sector research and development. *Direct Measures 2003*, EUR 20716.

difficulty finding an answer using today's technology. As a result, policy in general should be aimed at providing incentives for companies to address the grand challenges by means of emerging technologies. Considering the fact that large established organizations tend to focus on upholding their current market share on the basis of their installed-base, we believe that SMEs and entrepreneurial start-ups are more likely the kind of companies that will try and experiment the potential benefits of emerging technologies for societal challenges. Once the opportunity is identified, SMEs and entrepreneurial start-ups may be attractive candidates to be acquired by large established companies to be incorporated in their mainstream business. Market dissemination of emerging technologies through large established companies will be much quicker as it can build on the installed base of the production capacity, distribution channels, marketing knowledge available within established companies, see for example Figure 12.

The role of SMEs and entrepreneurial start-ups in experimenting emerging technologies and the importance of behavioral additionalities provide some directions on where policy instruments can intervene to stimulate responsible innovation. Consequently, we will discuss three areas for policy intervention where it is likely these considerations may materialize.

1. Interaction Between Regional Academe and SMEs

a. *The role of knowledge spill-overs*

Firms are continually influenced by the characteristics of the learning environment in which they operate. In this context, research of universities can be considered as extra-industry sources of knowledge.[3] Research institutes and universities in particular are sources of emerging technologies. However, they are, in general, not the kind of organizations that focus on technology development or the exploitation of technology in commercial markets. Large established companies have an interest in adopting scientific findings in their products and markets if it provides immediate benefits for them. SMEs and entrepreneurial start-ups are less likely than established companies to engage in contract or participate in research consortia. These SMEs and entrepreneurial start-ups tend to operate in niche markets and tend to

---

[3]Cohen, WM and Levinthal, DA (1990). Absorptive capacity: A new perspective on learning and innovation. *Administrative Science Quarterly*, 35(1), 128–152.

Rapid growth of electric vehicle (EV) fleet drives demand for fast-charging solutions.

Zurich, Switzerland, June 30, 2011 — ABB, the leading power and automation technology Group, announced today the acquisition of Epyon B.V., an early leader in electric vehicle charging infrastructure solutions focusing on direct current (DC) fast-charging stations and network charger software. The acquisition is in line with ABB's strategy to expand its global offering of electric vehicle infrastructure solutions.

"This acquisition gives ABB access to competitive products, key network management software, and a robust maintenance service business model, which ideally complements our own offering," said Ulrich Speisshofer, head of ABB's Discrete Automation and Motion division. Founded in 2005, Epyon is headquartered in Rijswijk, Netherlands, has an R&D center in Eindhoven and sales resources across Europe. Epyon's 50 staff worldwide will join ABB when the acquisition is completed.

"ABB's brand recognition and strong global presence will accelerate the growth of a combined Epyon — ABB offering, and provide access to key customers and partners," said Hans Streng, Epyon's CEO who led the company over the last year and who will stay as an experienced industrial leader of the combined business. "Epyon's existing business is complemented by ABB's strong power electronics platform, global manufacturing footprint as well as its supply, marketing and service network."

Figure 12. Press Release: ABB acquires Epyon to expand offering in EV charging infrastructure.[4]

use scientific findings which are not suitable for addressing large amounts of customers in established and mature markets. Nevertheless, these niche markets and emerging markets are the places where emerging technologies can be experimented and once they seem to become attractive they can be disseminated to larger markets with the help of large established companies. Policy instruments can help these processes by providing support to increase the interaction between SMEs and entrepreneurial start-ups with

---

[4]www.epyonpower.com/pdf/ABB-acquires-Epyon-2011-07-11.pdf.

research institutes and universities. In addition, since emerging technologies are highly uncertain with regards to the technical and market feasibility it is important to keep the innovation process flexible and open. As such, opportunities identified in various areas can be addressed and the likelihood of the technology providing benefit in the end will increase as compared to a narrower path of innovation in a closed innovation model.[5] Knowledge spill-overs are important to identify entrepreneurial opportunities with emerging technologies as well are the behavioral additionalities. In that respect, policy instruments could contribute to it by providing support for interaction between regional SMEs and academe. The support could be based on funding of project between academe and small companies, but the government could act as matchmaker or broker within the regional network of companies and academe, and thereby bring together parties which would not meet otherwise. The latter is aimed at increasing the behavioral additionalities of support and stimulates companies to look beyond the current set of activities.

2. Interaction Between SMEs from Different Sectors

Following the first policy instrument, policy makers can also provide benefit to SMEs and entrepreneurial start-ups by analyzing the current set of projects and programs they are involved in. Many times, public support is provided to a consortium of entrepreneurial start-ups, SMEs, incumbents and research institutes in order to further develop a technology. This technology might not only be of interest to the actors involved in the consortium but to other actors as well. The actors in the consortium might not look for exploitation of their technology beyond the market for various valid reasons. One is that their main focus is on their current market and dissemination to other companies could harm the competitive position they have built so carefully. However, adoption of the technology in other markets might not be detrimental to the competitive position immediately and may provide opportunities to the consortium as well because they can learn from applying technology in a broader set of application. The second reason is that organizations inside the consortium are focusing on meeting the project objectives and deadlines. They have little time to look beyond the

---

[5]Chesbrough, HW (2003). The era of open innovation. *MIT Sloan Management Review*, 44(3), 34–41.

current application they are aiming at and therefore, overlook possibilities of the technologies in other market sectors. The public agency responsible for the funding of projects and the coordination of the project programs, has more information on the kinds of technologies being developed and may signal similar developments in various sectors. By providing support programs that link the companies together across sectors, the dissemination and adoption of emerging technologies might be helped.

3. Role of Transnational Interaction Between SMEs and Technology Transfer Offices Located at Universities

Both the regional instruments to increase the interaction and knowledge spill-overs between academe and small companies and instruments to increase the brokerage between companies across sectors can be raised to the level of transnational collaboration.

In various clusters surrounding universities, we can identify communities of practice with individuals that interact because of their shared interests and common practices, as well as usage of the same tools and products.[6,7] However, the companies and people that are core members of the community can get trapped in the prevailing operations of business within their current task environment[8] and thus, are averse to discard existing knowledge and practices from other task environments. Therefore, those core members tend to ignore the potential contributions of new ideas from outside.[9] Various studies have pointed on the importance of transfer and

---

[6]Van Maanen, J and Barley, S (1984). Occupational communities: Culture and control in organizations. In Staw, BM and Cummings, LL (Eds.), *Research in Organizational Behavior*, Vol. 6, pp. 287–365. Greenwich, CT: JAI Press.

[7]Wellman, B, Salaff, J, Dimitrova, D, Garton, L, Gulia, M and Haythornthwaite, C (1996). Computer networks as social networks: Collaborative work, telework, and virtual community. *Annual Review of Sociology*, 22, 213–238.

[8]Gargiulo, M and M Benassi (2000). Trapped in your own net? Network cohesion, structural holes, and the adaptation of social capital. *Organizational Science*, 11, 183–196.

[9]Schilling, MA (2005). A "small-world" network model of cognitive insight. *Creativity Research Journal*, 17(2–3), 131–154.

sharing of knowledge between regions (cross-boundary) in these university-industry linkages.[10,11] Policy support, in particular at the EU level, could be aimed to increase the transnational transfer and allow for smoother dissemination of knowledge being generated at a university in one country and exploited within companies in another country.

4. Key Responsible Innovation Policy Barriers

The previous sections has identified the importance of interaction between academe and SMEs and entrepreneurial start-ups in order to allow for more emerging technologies to flourish in various product markets and an intent to address the grand challenges of society. The various policy instruments can increase the interaction between academe and SMEs and entrepreneurial start-ups, however, it is as much as important to understand the limitations and issues that are restricting the development of effective policies for responsible innovation. These include:

Supply side barriers

- Inadequate levels of responsible innovation research (apart from a handful of leading universities);
- Lack of structured coordination of existing research programs;
- Weak linkages between current responsible innovation research and market; and
- Inadequate skills base at a policy level.

Demand side barriers

- Market prices currently disincentives responsible innovation in some sectors (externalities);
- Demand side measures are too weak to drive responsible innovation, e.g. procurement; and

---

[10]Dahlander, L and Frederiksen, L (2012). The core and cosmopolitans: A relational view of innovation in user communities. *Organization Science*, 23(4), 988–1007.

[11]Tortoriello, M and Krackhardt, D (2010). Activating cross-boundary knowledge: The role of Simmelian ties in the generation of innovations. *Academic Management Journal*, 53(1), 167–181.

- Lack of appropriate and credible information on the value of responsible innovation.

Horizontal barriers

- Governance problems related to responsible innovation (complexity);
- Difficulty in providing and accessing responsible innovation finance;
- Unfavorable global conditions for responsible innovation (emerging market dynamics);
- Unused potential for eco-innovation in developed and developing countries; and
- Imbalance of responsible innovation capabilities across EU member states (and global supply chains).

The Lund Declaration (under the 2009 Swedish Presidency of the EU) combined and brought clarity to several important aspects of how science, technology and innovation can address these grand challenges. According to the Lund Declaration, "European research must focus on the grand challenges of our time moving beyond current rigid thematic approaches. This calls for a new deal among European institutions and Member States, in which European and national instruments are well aligned and cooperation builds transparency and trust. Identifying and responding to grand challenges should involve stakeholders from both public and private sectors in transparent processes taking into account the global dimension."

Interestingly, the Lund Declaration outlines the need to address these challenges through solutions. It suggests that the "challenges must turn into sustainable solutions in areas such as global warming, tightening supplies of energy, water and food, ageing societies, public health, pandemics and security. It must tackle the overarching challenge of turning Europe into an eco-efficient economy."

Furthermore, it is important to note that responsibility issues are highly interlinked as we discussed in Chapter 3 surrounding the concept of responsible innovation. When trying to increase the value of one of Brundtland's pillars it may happen that the value at another pillar is affected and it might be even detrimental to another dimension. Similarly, it would be beneficial to investigate how to uphold responsible innovation not because of sanctioning but because of positive incentive mechanisms. That is how to convert the mechanism of sanctioning into incentives that invites companies to further investigate the potential of emerging technologies and identify opportunities to solve the grand challenges. As such it is directly linked to the self-interest of the companies involved.

Another important consideration is the role of policy-makers is to provide a regulatory framework and infrastructure that allows including the conceptualization of responsible innovation into various disciplinary areas. Some ideas that are mentioned to include these are aimed at bringing professionals from diverse backgrounds together and use their expertise to contribute to responsible innovation issues:

- Raise awareness about responsible innovation among key actors;
- To be able to realize that responsible innovation are very context/dependent and need specific attention of individuals with local knowledge and expertise;
- Encourage reflexivity among the key actors;
- To establish a forum for stakeholder involvement where they exchange their experience and ideas and express their views on future developments;
- Provide a regulatory framework which will support responsible innovation as well as technological impact and technological forecasting; and
- Develop appropriate tools and methods to identify and address responsible innovation within the innovation process. Communication of this is important for the successful acknowledgement of responsibilities and the related sharing of good practice.

  - ➤ That is to collect, develop and communicate methodological, procedural and substantive aspects of responsible innovation;
  - ➤ Develop a platform for a public repository and dissemination of knowledge concerning responsible innovation;
  - ➤ Provide examples and case studies; and
  - ➤ To provide an early warning system for issues that may require legislation.

- To engage proactively in developing legal solutions to foreseeable problems that are likely to arise from emerging technologies; and
- Provide positive incentives to engage with issues of responsibility in innovation and emerging technologies.

5

RESPONSIBLE INNOVATION WITHIN RESEARCH AND EDUCATION

The preceding chapters have demonstrated the importance of responsible innovation as a management approach to the innovation process and the organization as a whole, in order to achieve positive results. These concern both the organization's performance as well as its impact on society. In some cases, a successful responsible innovation strategy can also contribute towards addressing some of the grand challenges of society. In order to overcome the problems facing us today, a new approach and perspective is needed, taking us beyond existing frameworks. Emerging technologies and entrepreneurial behavior are critical factors for exploring potential solutions, while remaining aware of the direct and indirect impacts which resulting innovations can have.

It is important to communicate these viewpoints not only to SME and entrepreneurial companies but also to policy-makers, academic researchers and scholars. Both research projects and teaching programs conducted at universities can benefit significantly from including the concept of responsible innovation within their programs. In terms of research programs, an inclusion of the ideas surrounding responsible innovation will eventually benefit those who will be either impacted by the results of the research or using the latter. Similarly, familiarizing students with the responsible innovation concept throughout their studies will help them acquire the certain mindset necessary to pursue their projects later on, with regards to the development of new products and services, or even sustainable business models, for instance. Indeed, these will have more chances of success if they are conducted in light of the objectives of responsibility and performance through innovation, which will in turn greatly benefit the organization.

While the roots of the concept of responsible innovation can be found in Brundtland's sustainability agenda, it has been further refined by contributions from various academic disciplines. Humanities and philosophy in particular have made a significant contribution to these conceptual theories. This multidisciplinary approach has proved to be both challenging and effective in terms of the depth with which the concept was analyzed from differing perspectives to include the varying stakes and objectives of all disciplines involved.

1. Research Grants

A long-standing characteristic of the academic community is the importance placed upon the number and impact of publications produced by researchers. As such, research incentives are generally geared towards achieving a greater number of published material, aimed at generating more impact. Research grants are very important to relieve researchers from heavy teaching obligations and provide them with the data necessary for future publications. A discussion has recently emerged about the third mission of academic staff and universities, that is, besides the teaching of students and the conducting of research: academic staff should become more active in the dissemination of their research findings and aim towards providing greater benefit for society as a whole through this research. Such benefit can be in the form of contribution toward the development of innovative products and services for individual organizations, or can even serve a group of society that may be negatively affected by an innovation. This third mission represents the dissemination of research findings and the 'valorization' of research which is a central part of the connection between the elements of the Triple Helix of 'university–industry–government.'[1] It has also led to the increasing importance of discussing and defending any research in terms of its impact and benefit for society. This issue surfaces especially when applying for research grants. Applications for the latter generally include a section for explaining how the social implications of the scientific work will be addressed. This may sometimes be accompanied by an additional paragraph suggesting the potential ways in which

---

[1] Etzkowitz, H (2008). *The Triple Helix: University–Industry–Government Innovation in Action.* London: Routledge.

the scientific findings can be commercially exploited. In animal research and medicine, these sections have traditionally been allocated great weight in terms of importance and relevance. In these cases, the potential saving of lives unquestionably provides good grounds for arguing the need and urgency to fund the research project at hand, while national regulations demands are also increasingly inquisitive and demanding of concrete evidence regarding the protection of animals from testing or experimenting practices. However, this part is currently considered of minor importance and relevance for a large number of research projects in other sectors.

The EU Commission has expressed its intention to place more emphasis on the degree of care taken with regards to the responsibility of the research project. Responsible research and innovation is a term which is increasingly present within the EU Commission, especially in the context of Horizon 2020, which has evidently aroused the interest of various research groups across universities, institutes, think-tanks and private companies. A potential area of improvement for grant applications in the future could be an added requirement section for a more detailed declaration of value, defining exactly what value is being provided, who is reaping the benefits of the scientific finding and an identification of potential positive and negative impacts of the project on society, with a set of potential measures to address adverse consequences. A further feature could include a declaration of compliance detailing how to keep track of the normative scheme, outlining the outcomes and the potential repercussions on the wider circle of stakeholders. It is important to understand the ways in which these additional requirements would impact both the research project applicant as well as the research subsidizer; in the case of the former, a more thorough understanding of the project and its potential impacts would be required along with a set of measures to be implemented for monitoring unforeseen consequences as the project pans out. Furthermore, the research program manager may need to collaborate with expert groups, complementing their own skills and expertise, to monitor impacts and conduct stakeholder analyses more precisely. In the case of the research subsidizer, a more sophisticated method of evaluation and a more detailed system for allocating research grants would need to be designed and implemented. Both universities and subsidy agents have little experience in these matters for the moment, highlighting the need for exemplary cases and experience to be collected over the coming years.

2. Teaching Programs

The teaching of responsible innovation should eventually replace the previous 'classic' innovation courses being taught at universities. The largest mechanism of knowledge transfer between universities and the business environment is by far the teaching of students. The latter should be taught that innovating and launching new products and services is not necessarily socially, economically or environmentally benign. As discussed previously, a responsible innovation strategy can be integrated in large multinationals as well as SMEs. In fact, the smaller structures and potentially greater flexibility of SMEs and start-ups may facilitate the integration of such a strategy for sharpening their competitive edge and these may even be able to dedicate a whole part of their innovation activities towards addressing societal grand challenges. Thus, the potential integration of responsible innovation in teaching programs is largely justified.

Innovation management and entrepreneurship teaching programs will greatly benefit from the added dimension of responsibility, which provides added insights and understandings regarding the value of innovation both within an organization, as within the wider society. The responsible innovation theories also place great emphasis on the need for multidisciplinary teams, which can also provide added value for the design and content of teaching programs. Such programs should aim at drawing from strategies to enhance the capacity of researchers and students while encouraging them to consider the commercial application of their research, its impacts and relevance in new and existing businesses. These can also feed into existing training programs on responsible innovation.

Similarly, transnational collaboration between SME and universities across regional and national boundaries should be encouraged through initiatives along two main axes of collaboration: course material and student exchanges. Co-designing and exchanging selected course materials and case studies will help incorporate various perspectives on the topic of responsible innovation. Including knowledge about emerging technologies and opportunities for solving societal grand challenges into these courses will turn them into an invaluable source of information for universities and members of the KARIM. The universities within the KARIM program will be able to share transnational access to existing training, initially allowing students and staff from each of the partner universities (and subsequently the wider KARIM network) to have the opportunity to gain training in any one of the member institutions.

a.　*Challenges for including responsible innovation*

Including responsible innovation within educational programs presents several challenges. These mainly emerge from the fact that the concept requires an appreciation and understanding of ethics and philosophy as well as a broader orientation towards the stakeholders who need to be considered throughout the development of innovation projects. Social science students from programs such as sociology, economics, business administration, among others, may find it easier to include such elements and engage in a multidisciplinary approach when discussing stakeholder involvement. However, engineering students mainly draw their core experience from subjects such as mechanical engineering, physics and life sciences. While their experience in these disciplines can lead to research activities potentially resulting in the application of technology in commercial settings, they generally lack experience in the commercialization of innovation. Moreover, engineering graduates are traditionally expected to work by themselves or with collaborators sharing the same educational and training background, which means that they are not used to including various stakeholders that may be positively or negatively affected by their innovation. As a result, it seems that addressing responsible innovation in third-level curricula should be discussed in terms of process, content and skills.

Firstly, with regards to the process, it is necessary to gain a more thorough and precise understanding with regards to the steps required for translating the concept of responsible innovation into the process of technological and commercial application. This process is generally characterized by its non-linear path of progress along which many, often unforeseen, issues arise which might affect the direction of the new innovation. A better understanding of the process itself, the basis from which it was developed and the issues it aims to address will maximize students' management ability with regards to such innovation projects. Indeed, they will acquire the capacity to think about the wider social, economic and environmental factors which may be affected both by the development process as by the finished new product or service. They will thus be better able to identify and engage relevant stakeholders in addressing upcoming issues throughout the development phases.

Secondly, it comes as no surprise that content needs to be carefully addressed with regards to the elements to be included when teaching about the practice of responsible innovation. Case studies and experiential learning methodologies are used across a wide variety of complex subjects and disciplines with the aim of reproducing a 'real life' type of environment for students, governed by various factors including intense market pressure, within which difficult decisions must be made. However, it is still difficult to separate oneself completely from an anecdotal approach and engage in a fully generic one with such practical exercises. The anecdotal approach provides a useful method for understanding the complexity and nature of the dynamics at play when involving stakeholders at crucial stages of the innovation process. Indeed, the procedure of bringing diverging interests together and balancing these in order to steer the innovation in the right direction represents a certain level of risk which should not be underestimated. At the same time, a more generic understanding of key areas of concern in combination with the more anecdotal case study examples is necessary to generalize the issues and apply them to other types of innovations, organizations and sectors. This would once again allow a better understanding of the dynamics of responsible innovation.

Thirdly, a focus on managerial and entrepreneurial behavior skills should make up a key part of responsible innovation courses at third level. For instance, presentation skills need to be sharpened and adapted for catching the attention of specific target audiences, especially in terms of engaging new stakeholders from differing backgrounds and sectors, whose cognitive experiences and communication skills vary widely. Furthermore, effective persuading, negotiating and influencing skills are essential in order to conduct productive debates as part of the innovation process, aiming to meet agreements or resolve dilemmas as issues arise among stakeholders at various stages of development. Therefore, the effective responsible innovation pedagogy requires both a mastering of the necessary skills for convincing stakeholders, investors and partners to collaborate on the one hand and a display of the marketing skills to attract and gain support for the innovation on the other. The transfer of such skills will help students understand the stakes of dealing in uncertain environments with a wide variety of actors, especially in terms of innovation. They will be trained to adapt their own behavior for dealing with stakeholders (and their diverging interests), motivating employees, planning or orchestrating technological innovation and developing new business plans.

As responsible innovation is a complex topic, it requires a multiplex pedagogical approach. Traditional approaches of learning, which apply for instance to engineering or similar mathematics-based courses, focus on concrete results and relatively measurable outcomes. However, the process of responsible innovation and the identification of critical issues require a more dynamic and often varied approach, as no situation resembles the other. As such, several solutions may even be identified to solve a single problem and each one may be as valuable and good as the other.

Engineering students are usually encouraged to develop a mindset that aims at developing a single best or optimal solution. Yet, responsible innovation requires an attitude which accepts the possibility that a more diverse set of outcomes may be perfectly acceptable and implementable for addressing a specific issue. Indeed, since responsible innovation is surrounded by uncertainty several different approaches may co-exist and be needed simultaneously. This therefore requires a different mindset to the one applicable in the pure scientific field. Acquiring the skills necessary to manage a responsible innovation process and implement the relevant mindset across an organization requires a specific attitude which is difficult to test by means of a written exam. Different pedagogical methods and tools, including case studies and real-life company project assignments are needed to reinforce the skills and theories learned in the classroom. In fact, class sessions require a more interactive approach, to ensure students are actively engaged in debates and are faced with practical problems, to help them put the theory into practice.

Finally, the level of importance of a particular issue may vary over the duration of the responsible innovation process and its eventual commercial application. It is thus critical to point out the particularity of the time issue to students; indeed certain issues will arise and be particularly relevant at specific stages of development of the innovation. They will therefore need to be addressed accordingly.

In summary, the following needs and constraints should be considered and understood:

- The dynamic setting in which responsible innovation operates and the uncertainty which characterizes its surrounding environment;
- The wide range of skills, expertise and techniques relevant for responsible innovation;
- The strategy and process needed for implementing responsible innovation;
- The articulation of the important issues and activities surrounding responsible innovation.

b.   *Including responsible innovation at various levels of education systems*

Traditionally, courses linked to the responsible innovation debate feature topics centered on safety, well-being, health, carbon footprint, and so on. These are discussed in terms of eco-design, user-centered innovation, life-cycle analysis or closed loop supply chains. Examples of applications include the design of medical devices, safety gear, living environment design, etc. Over the last couple of years, the benefits of a responsible approach to innovation have been recognized in terms of its contribution to creativity, the uncovering of new market opportunities and the development of new business models.

Awareness

Since responsible innovation is a difficult concept to understand, the phase of awareness would be to let students get familiar before including the philosophical or ethical debates and implications linked to the topic. The aim of this introductory phase would be to raise awareness among students with regards to the benefits of responsible innovation and the many business opportunities which may arise from implementing such a strategy and process. In order to be effective, this awareness session would need strong, concrete evidence of the advantages of responsible innovation illustrated by practical case studies demonstrating the inclusion of stakeholders, the questioning of direct and indirect impacts of the innovation. More importantly, the case study would show the challenges encountered and the benefits reaped by the organization as a whole. While case studies showing a positive correlation between the adoption of responsible innovation and the ultimate success of innovation would evidently be more impactful on both students and managers, certain 'failed attempts' case studies would also show the lessons learned to enrich the debate of this still relatively new concept. On the other hand, the 'success stories' would need to feature strong evidence of higher financial gains generated through responsible innovation, in order to explicitly demonstrate the advantages to all interested parties.

Inspiration

Following the awareness session, inspirational lectures provided by engineers, entrepreneurs and managers successfully engaging in responsible innovation would further contribute to illustrating the practicalities of the concept in a real business context. These industry leaders of responsible innovation would inspire students to follow in their footsteps and get involved in developing innovations which need to be at the service of citizens and society, not the other way around. The ensuing discussions and debates can then be based on these real life examples and focus on the issues encountered when engaging various stakeholders for instance or when changing production processes to use less rare earth minerals, switching to more sustainable materials or even developing new business models. Such discussions can include the critical analysis and review of certain tools, such as total cost ownership, which now covers social and environmental factors in its estimations.

Bachelor Level Education

Bachelor level students of general management or engineering subjects gain a general understanding of their topic throughout their initial third-level studies. Many universities offer an increasing amount of courses on sustainable engineering, social business models, corporate social responsibility and so on. There are also more and more ethics courses being integrated into engineering studies in order to address the responsibility of engineers to consider the impacts of their research and innovations on the user and society as a whole. Increasingly, case studies have been focusing on the different ways in which engineers, managers and whole organizations have addressed corporate social responsibility issues in the past; how these experiences have impacted their attitude towards stakeholder groups and what, they believe, are the areas for future improvement. Currently, the main focus of bachelor level studies is to provide students with an understanding of corporate social responsibility, the ethics of conducting business and engineering designs, as well as general topics related to innovation, creativity and business management. An introduction to the basis of the responsible innovation concept should however be part of curricula, as early on as possible. As such, students should be confronted with responsible innovation issues from the moment they receive lectures on innovation and its surrounding uncertainty.

Master Level Education

Courses at the Master level would generally include more discussion, reflection and elaboration on the concept of responsible innovation. At this level, specific lectures are developed to introduce the responsibility of managers with regards to the innovation and help students to gain the adequate perspective for identifying relevant stakeholders and communicating with them effectively. Courses on corporate social responsibility should not be confused with those on responsible innovation as the former will focus more on the specific department of a company which aims to generate social value and which is generally completely separated from the innovation department. Responsible innovation courses on the other hand, will take a look at the entire organization's commitment towards achieving responsibility through innovation and achieving innovation through responsibility, as a strategy and process. While subjects such as user-centered design, co-creation with clients and stakeholder analyses are usually included into core programs for economics and business administration, the responsible innovation programs should feature topics such as technology assessment, along with comparative analyses of the different types of the latter; techniques such as road mapping, scenario analyses and new methodologies developed by ongoing research, such as those developed by biomimicry for instance.

Furthermore, Master level programs should include a variety of organizational design lectures, where responsible innovation can be discussed in terms of new opportunities which need to be pursued with a different mindset and other heuristics to problem solving. Courses covering topics such as creativity, design-thinking, breaking with dominant logic, designing and building an organizational structure with procedures for finance, human resources development, etc. will all contribute to developing and enriching the multidisciplinary scope of the debate and concepts surrounding responsible innovation.

Engineering courses increasingly cover topics linked to emerging technologies, new materials, life cycle analyses, etc. The transfer of social and communication skills should also become a major part of these programs, previously considered to be 'purely scientific.' It is therefore likely that certain technical and scientific bases will cross over into business curricula, while some course components on skills for presenting, convincing, negotiating and consensus building will cross over into engineering programs.

As mentioned previously, all innovation courses should eventually be replaced by responsible innovation, in order to teach students from both social sciences and technical backgrounds, that the only way to innovate in today's society is to do so, responsibly.

Executive Courses

Any innovative organization operating would benefit greatly from an introduction to the philosophy which forms the basis for responsible innovation, before learning about the required strategy and process. At present, integrating responsible innovation lectures into executive courses would seem to be the most effective way of increasing its integration into industry. On the other hand, this requires significant organizational change which, realistically, will not happen overnight. However, it is no harm to raise the awareness of individual employees with regards to the impacts of their innovations and general business activities in order to provoke them into considering potential alternatives, which could be implemented over time. As such, it can be more impactful to begin such courses with a discussion centered on the philosophy of life, to get executive students thinking about their individual existence (beginning from the moment they were born) and their individual essence (gradually emerging through life and conditioned made by the many choices faced in relation to their responsibility), as suggested by the French philosopher, Jean-Paul Sartre. The reflection would then be steered towards questioning why we, as human beings, have an irrepressible need to develop, grow, change, adapt, reinvent ourselves, in other words: innovate. This would help guide these experienced students, whose thoughts may have been conditioned a certain way or another by their organization, to take a step back and question the very essence of their actions both in their personal life as in their professional life.

The next phase of the executive course would focus on the basics of innovation in a business context, which would then lead onto the analysis of innovations' impacts on social, economic and environmental factors. Following the presentation of the process required for implementing responsible innovation across an organization, the presentation of practical case studies by the very individuals who made it happen and were faced with the issues themselves would help convince students with regards to the possibility of making change happen. It is important to note the difference in target audience between Bachelor and Master level students and those in executive courses. Both groups will not be attracted by the same facts, nor will their attention be retained by the same pedagogical approach. Once again, this shows the relevance of applying responsible innovation to the education sector itself, regarding both contents and methods of approach and delivery.

6

ACHIEVING
RESPONSIBLE INNOVATION
AND OPTIMIZING
ON PERFORMANCE

Highlighting the importance of responsibility within innovation strategies is one thing, proving that it offers a competitive advantage in terms of creating value is another. Yet, the latter is a crucial argument in convincing companies to adopt such an approach. It is in itself relatively easy to justify a position of responsibility in an innovation context, just as it is to justify a position of sustainable development in an economic or organizational context. There is no opposition, nor are there opponents, nothing in fact can really harm such a project. Moreover, in light of the current context, everyone has their own speech prepared on the subject. Who is not responsible nowadays, if only through a couple of lines included into the annual activities report? What company do not have, even a snippet of facts on sustainable development in their presentation brochures? It has become an essential, if not expected, part of corporate communication. In the present day and age, we need to be responsible. Willingly or not, a company must have a responsible discourse ready. Ever since the recent financial crisis, everything has gained a responsible "coating." Advertisements are over-flowing with the term: "responsible" credit offers, "responsible" cars, nuclear energy has now become "responsible," yoghurts are "responsible," and so on. The message has been clearly received and understood by communication bodies: we must be responsible.

As it happens, very few of these offers actually turn out to be responsible. They mainly serve as communication tools to make the firm appear as being responsible, in line with the current trend. The underlying question is: why are we not responsible? Why do companies, managers develop pure communication strategies instead of developing actual responsible offers? Part of the answer is linked to the fact that preconceptions die hard and when faced with the question: "what brings real financial returns?" "Being responsible" is rarely understood as a response. "Responsibility" is rarely suggested as the solution to the development and growth of the company. Responsibility, sustainable development along with other notions of this kind are usually perceived as an obstacle, a hindrance to business performance. This is partly true since all of these dimensions have so far been perceived as sources of cost (recycling, compliance with legislations) or as obstacles (validation by external agencies for market launch, etc.).

This is perhaps the most important argument of our discussion: throughout the innovation process, how to convince a company, a manager, a CEO to implement a responsibility, which is considered, seen, understood as an obstacle? Only one answer is possible: induced performance. To be clear, raising awareness does not suffice to provoke change on such a large scale. While it could work for some managers, it is not enough due to the challenges and objectives facing the latter. These issues differ widely from the ones of responsibility by definition. The manager is faced with shareholders, banks, employees, performances, competitors, short-term objectives, etc. Responsibility is traditionally tainted with a different kind of message: long term, citizen, cost, anticipation, etc.

The only notion which can appeal to the manager is that of performance. If the integration of responsibility, no matter what shape or form, is source of performance, then all corporate leaders will actively open their ears, conscience, agenda, meetings, etc. Such is the aim of this chapter: to fight against pre-conceived ideas and to show that responsibility can clearly be a source of innovation, performance, competitiveness.

Michael Porter shares this mindset when he claims that corporate social responsibility has become "a religion filled with priests, in which there is no need for evidence or theory. Too many academics and business managers are satisfied with the 'good feeling' as argument. Much corporate philanthropy is driven by top management's personal beliefs. It is their pet project. And almost all corporate philanthropy is about brand enhancement and gaining a reputation as a positive citizen. [...]

I disagree completely. [...] Companies need to move away from defensive actions into a pro-active integration of social initiatives into business competitive strategy."[1] Porter suggests that social responsibility can only be effective in a "cost-benefit" context for the firm. Investing in responsibility must have the same characteristics, speak the same language in order to attract the attention of corporate leaders. It is necessary to be wary of these so-called Corporate social responsibility (CSR) "priests" for instance, who provide feel-good speeches which will never be followed through with corporate strategies as long as all issues at stake are not understood by all people involved. We shall now see what methods, actions and strategies allow combining responsibility and economic performance.

1. Applying Disruptive Innovation to the Social Sector

Although this opening argument concerns a more social than a responsible type of innovation as we understand it, it is nevertheless important as it shows the relationship between performance, efficiency and responsibility. Thus, there is no conflict between social responsibility and benefits. In addition, the following three examples will emphasize two critical points at this stage: an innovation is not always of a technological nature, nor does it always have to be an add-on or improvement to an existing offer. The aim, above all is to meet a need which has either not yet been addressed or is being addressed inappropriately.

Foundations of the Catalytic Model: As its name implies, a disruptive innovation through its radical proposition and contrary to an incremental innovation, generally provokes a disruption or shock to the market or position once it is launched. This can be through an offer, a product or the entry into a new market. Christensen's catalytic innovation model shares these characteristics of a disruptive innovation, underlining the benefits for actors which arise from outside of the pre-established framework. The catalytic innovation differs from the disruptive innovation by its particular relevance and application to the social sector (health, education, training,

---

[1]Porter, M (2003). CSR — A religion with too many priests? *European Business Forum, Interview with Mette Morsig* (Online), 15 (Autumn). Available at http://www.fsg.org/Portals/0/Uploads/Documents/PDF/CSR_Religion_with_Too_Many_Priests.pdf?cpgn=WP%20DL%20-%20CSR%20-%20A%20Religion%20With%20too%20Many%20Priests. (accessed on March 13, 2013).

Catalytic Model ╲ ╲ ╲ ╲ ╲ Innovation	Reduce and replicate: do less but better	Meet a need which, up until now, was either very 'badly met' (with complex solution), or not met enough (insufficient solutions available)	Provide a service which is more simple, less expensive, more affordable	Create financial, human and sharable resources	Understand the fact that these needs are often ignored, discouraged by the actors already in place
Investing in Health Insurance		X	X	X	X
Investing in Education	X		X	X	
Investing in Economic Development		X	X	X	

Figure 13. An application of the catalytic model to innovation across three different sectors.[2]

etc.). As represented in Figure 13, the five fundamental pillars which provide the basis for the catalytic model are as follows:

• Reduce and replicate: do less but better;
• Meet a need which, up until now, was either very "badly met" (with complex solution) or not provide with enough solutions;
• Provide a service which is more simple, less expensive, more affordable;
• Create financial, human and sharable resources; and
• Understand the fact that these needs are often ignored, discouraged by the actors already in place.

2. Investing in Health Insurance

The Freelancers Union[3] organization developed a radically innovative offer called low cost health insurance, along with other services aimed at

---

[2]Pavie, X (2012). *Innovation responsable. Stratégie et levier de croissance des organisations.* Paris: Eyrolles.
[3]Available at www.freelancersunion.org.

independent workers, part-time employees, individuals on precarious short-term contracts based in New York, who cannot afford health insurance. The organization provides insurance offers at rates which are 30% to 40% lower than the individual insurance plans available and are also more adapted to suit the specificities of the target group. Indeed, actuarial analyses showed that these types of employees have generally low exposure to risks and have very precise needs. Thus, an offer was specifically developed to suit that particular category of individuals, thereby, also guaranteeing an adjusted price. The competitive advantage generated by Freelancers Union is very significant since competitors are not able to match this offer; it would make no sense in this case to multiply this offer and only one is required to meet the needs of this target group.

3.   Investing in Education

The increasingly wide spread of the English language across the world has developed at the expense of other languages on school curricula. In fact, the cost of recruiting teachers of languages whose demand by students is decreasing is becoming too high to be borne by the schools. However, instead of stopping classes of these less "popular" languages, the Online Classes organization has developed a web-based language learning facility, thereby making it available all over the world. The website brings together 40,000 students from 37 states in North America, all particularly motivated and diligent as they feel part of a greater project for promoting, developing and preserving languages other than English.

4.   Investing in Economic Developments

The healthcare system in Kenya is highly hierarchical, complex and urban. Thus, 80% of practitioners are based in the cities while 70% of the population lives in rural areas. This situation makes it very difficult to access health care services, which was part of the reason for HealthStore Foundation[4] to train local residents to deliver basic medical care. By transferring basic medical knowledge and supplying the main healthcare equipment, the foundation provided a means of lowering the average cost of consulting from $3 to 50 cents a visit.

---

[4] Available at www.cfwshops.org.

5. Integrating Responsibility: A Source of Innovation and Performance

A study carried out by Lopez-Perez *et al.* which focused on the relationship between the responsibility and competitiveness of 95 European firms showed that a corporate social responsibility strategy generally and an integration of responsibility into the innovation process is as much a factor of competitiveness as it is one of profit.[5]

Indeed, the study aimed at comparing the performance of firms from the Dow Jones Sustainable Index (DJSI) and the Dow Jones Global Index (DJGI) in terms of three categories:

— The company's attitude towards responsibility;
— The innovation strategy and practices;
— The relationship between responsibility and innovation.

A firm needs to fulfill a certain number of criteria in order to be part of the Dow Jones Sustainable Index. These are categorized into three dimensions, namely economic (e.g. Risk and crisis management, company governance); environmental (e.g. Ecological efficiency, environmental reporting) and social (e.g. Development of human capital, talent attraction and retention). These criteria cannot be overlooked by firms wishing to implement a policy of responsibility throughout the organization. On the other hand, companies from the Dow Jones Global Index do not need to conform to such criteria of responsibility. The whole point of the study therefore lies in comparing the performance of companies which take into account responsible practices with those which do not explicitly follow such a strategy. Five hypotheses were created in order to analyze whether the degree responsibility of a company is a factor of profit or whether on the contrary it hinders performance:

Hypothesis 1: Companies which have a responsible approach to business have a greater advantage to those which do not;

Hypothesis 2: A responsible strategy has a positive effect on the firm's financial results;

---

[5]Lopez-Perez, V, Perez-Lopez, C and Rodriguez-Ariza, L (2007). The opinion of European companies on corporate social responsibility and its relation to innovation. *Issues in Social and Environmental Accounting*, 1(2), 276–295.

Hypothesis 3: Companies which have a responsible approach to business integrate environmental aspects into their strategy;

Hypothesis 4: Companies which follow a responsible approach to business generate more incremental than radical innovations;

Hypothesis 5: A responsible approach to business influences the innovation strategy.

These hypotheses were then tested through a series of interviews, questionnaires, meetings with companies from both the DJSI and DJGI. The results of the study speak for themselves as a comparative statistics analysis helped derive several crucial lessons:

1. DJSI companies generally present a greater level of alignment with topics linked to responsibility in general and particularly with responsible innovation;
2. Implementing a responsible approach is a strategic advantage and influences innovation mechanisms and strategies about to be put into practice. In other words, the choice between following a policy of incremental or breakthrough innovation practices is indeed different. If the company wishes to adopt both, a different type of organization is needed, meaning the degree of responsibility and the type of process needed also differs;
3. An integration of responsibility across an organization increases its competitive advantage, with satisfactory results in the short and long term, while also meeting the demands and requirements of stakeholders in a responsible manner. Therefore, adopting such a policy benefits all actors, i.e. customers, partners, suppliers, etc.
4. Companies considered that integrating responsibility not only creates innovation and value in the long term, but also contributes to business development;
5. These responsible practices therefore show that an integration of responsibility impacts on the company's global strategy, its innovation strategy and optimizes the innovation process. Such strategies are only made effective by the whole company's commitment, from the top down, to being responsible.

6. Critical Analysis of the Dow Jones Sustainable Index

The DJSI is a global index for measuring a company's level of responsibility. It takes into account economic aspects (governance, crisis management, codes of conduct, etc.), environmental behavior (sustainable development, regulation, etc.) and social elements (human capital development, training, etc.). However, the DJSI does not take into account the company's ultimate goal or purpose. This brings us back to the difference between social innovation and responsible innovation. Indeed, it may seem surprising to consider that companies such as British American Tobacco, Heineken, Ladbroker, Total, GlaxoSmithKline are part of the DJSI. The latter therefore understands the notion of responsibility as a company's willingness to conform to its responsibilities. Knowing if one should smoke, drive a Diesel car, drink beer, place bets on football matches are considerations of responsibility which do not only concern the firm. In this regard, citizens also have a share of responsibility: they are ultimately the ones to decide whether to consume or not, to buy or not, to use or not.[6]

IBM sought to identify best practices and effective strategies of those companies that are well on their way in their journey toward becoming a sustainable enterprise. Their research has led them to conclude the three S's of sustainability and responsibility: Strategy, Synergy and Significance.

The research found that organizations need to establish and communicate a vision of sustainability through a well-defined strategy. This fact is directly applicable to the integration of a vision of responsibility within the organization, which will be in line with its performance objectives. Companies need a path toward articulating such a vision, accompanied by an appropriate executive sponsorship and the right level of leadership attention and commitment.

According to the study, the importance of sustainability programs for the organization's overall health and wealth is partly reflected by its report system directly aimed at the CEO. The CEO works hand-in-hand with the Chief Sustainability Officer (CSO), who in turn ensures that the sustainability strategy is optimized and fully integrated into the business planning model. Last but not least, the CSO ensures the CEO and other C-level executives and senior managers remain engaged throughout the process, while also managing the resource and plan contention effectively and putting the appropriate responsibility and accountability models into place.[7]

---

[6]Pavie, X (2012). *Innovation responsable. Stratégie et levier de croissance des organisations.* Paris: Eyrolles.

[7]Butner, K (2011). Driving performance through sustainability: Strategy, synergy and significance. *IBM Global Business Services* (Online). Available at ftp:// public.dhe.ibm.com/common/ssi/ecm/en/gbe03414usen/GBE03414USEN.PDF. Accessed on March 13, 2013.

What parts of your organization participate in your sustainability program?

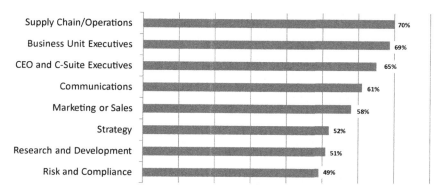

IBM Institute for Business Value and Esty Environmental Partners Sustainability Research Study (2011)

Figure 14.   Organizational alignment for sustainability program.

From Figure 14, we can deduce that the implementation of a responsible innovation strategy serves as a logical progression to a Sustainability Program, as it would cause the participation of the three lowest parts of the organization (namely "Strategy," "Research and Development" and "Risk and Compliance") to increase their implication. We have seen that responsible innovation involves the implementation of responsible practices throughout the organization as a whole and therefore becomes an essential part of the strategy. It also becomes an integral part of research and development, both in terms of creating new innovation projects as well as linking with research needs in terms of risks surrounding these projects.

Effective monitoring and measurement systems adaptable and applicable to companies across various industries are key as different programs are under way and being evaluated according to differing criteria. While many companies are embracing a monitoring and measurement agenda in the implementation of sustainability practices, calculating impacts for instance on various environmental factors, there is still room for improvement. This applies in the case of deploying responsible innovation practices: leaders need to create a synergy between the various initiatives being carried out. In fact, the study shows that innovators are generally adept at incorporating sustainability benefits into the customer value proposition. This could therefore be considered as a stepping stone towards achieving responsible innovation.

The organization as a whole needs to comprehend the significance behind adopting principles of sustainability and in turn, responsible-innovation. If we consider that over two-thirds of the business leaders polled and interviewed are focusing on sustainability initiatives to create new revenue streams and over half believe that their companies' sustainability activities are already giving them an advantage over their top competitors (IBM Institute for Value Analysis, 2011),[8] adopting a responsible innovation strategy as a driver for growth makes perfect sense.

Despite the increasing implementation of sustainability programs through common initiatives linked to cutting down carbon emissions, reducing waste and so on, companies have yet to understand that a strategy can only be sustainable if it addresses the interests of all stakeholders. This means not only taking into account the needs of investors, employees and customers, but also governments, NGOs and society as a whole.[9]

A recent study conducted by Eccles and Serafeim[10] analyzed the trade-offs between the financial performance of a firm and that of ESG dimensions. While capital markets do not reward firms for integrating ESG programs that fail to enhance financial performance, harsh penalties can also ensue for ignoring these. From the bad press and that followed revelations of Foxconn's dreadful working conditions in its manufacturing factories for Apple in China which eventually halved its market cap to BP's managerial and engineering disaster on its Deepwater Horizon oil rig in the Gulf of Mexico, there are countless industry examples of the consequences for prioritizing financial over ESG performance.

Figure 15 developed throughout this study[11] — involving interviews, surveys and field research with hundreds of companies across numerous sectors — presents a conceptual model of the complex relationship between the firm's financial objectives and ESG performance. Financial performance is plotted on the Y-axis, while ESG performance is represented

---

[8]Driving performance through sustainability: Strategy, synergy and significance (2011). Executive report, IBM Global Business Services (Online). Available at: ftp://public.dhe.ibm.com/common/ssi/ecm/en/gbe03414usen/GBE03414USEN.PDF. (accessed on March 13, 2013).

[9]Eccles, RG and Serafeim, G (2013). The performance frontier: Innovating for a sustainable strategy. *Harvard Business Review*, 91(5), 50–60.

[10]*Ibid.*

[11]*Ibid.*

Without substantial innovation, the financial performance of firms declines as their ESG performance improves. New products, processes and business models need to be created in order to improve both kinds of performance.

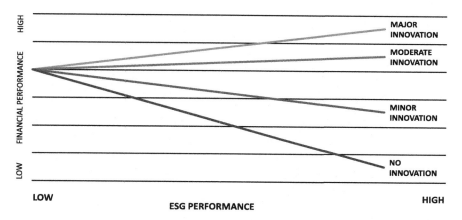

Figure 15.   The performance frontier.[12]

on the X-axis. The slope of a line depicts the relationship between financial and ESG performance. The steeper the downward slope, the greater the negative impact a firm's ESG improvements have on financial performance. A steeper upward slope reveals a greater positive impact following such improvements. Eccles and Serafeim refer to this as the "Performance Frontier."

We suggest that adopting a responsible innovation strategy would help solve issues linked to the performance frontier by creating value for the firm, while monitoring the impacts that such innovation projects have on social, economic and environmental factors. A responsible innovation strategy goes even further by anticipating potential, unknown impacts through creating a set of hypotheses to be tested post-launch.

The integration of responsibility therefore impacts the organization's strategy in ways which will depend on the firm's very structure and the

---

[12]Eccles, RG and Serafeim, G (2013). The performance frontier: Innovating for sustainable strategy. *Harvard Business Review*, 91(5), 50–60.

industry it operates in. However, by integrating responsibility at the heart of its offer, the company acquires a competitive advantage as part of its very DNA, making it very difficult for rivals to compete. Starbucks is an interesting example in this case, as competitors such as Dunkin' Donuts, Columbus Café or even Coffee and Beans continually need to catch up by aligning themselves to the industry leader, failing however to reach its leading standards (please see Starbucks case study in Appendix).

7. The Importance of Governance

How can we give innovation the space and freedom it needs without slowing it down, while at the same time monitoring it and its potential impacts? What kind of governance would meet these requirements? What possible legal regulations could be applied?

The main issue linked to the uncertainty surrounding innovation is the interdependency between time and diffusion. As a new technology is launched onto the market, its deployment happens in a length of time completely separate to the time required to evaluate the risks involved. Hence, it took a certain number of years for the potential health risks resulting from the use of mobile phones to be uncovered following the initial launch of the devices. It is this very time gap which makes up one of the major issues at stake at the heart of the responsible innovation concept. It portrays precisely the fundamental importance of monitoring the evolution of innovations, their possible consequences and the need for this to be carried out by an external governing body, capable of making the obliging decision to remove it from the market if needed.

A typical example would be the case of asbestos, widely used by manufacturers at the end of the 19th century due to its resistance to heat, tension, chemical and electrical aggressions and its strong absorption capacity. Despite clearly identifying the significant dangers of asbestos at the beginning of the 20th century, lobbying committees financed by manufacturing groups in favor of the asbestos were formed and the use of the chemical was only banned by the mid 1980s–1990s in various countries.[13] It is only in 2005 that a European directive banning the use of asbestos in all EU-member states is issued. The use of asbestos was not condemnable at an

---

[13]Lenglet, R (1996). *L'Affaire de l'amiante*. Paris: La Découverte Enquêtes.

earlier stage due to the lack of precise information concerning its adverse effects. Nevertheless, without the presence of an external governance body, as soon as the problems arose, the major manufacturing groups had the power to keep their innovation on the market. A system of governance, stronger regulations or a monitoring process linked to the innovation process implemented by an independent, yet authoritative body could have very possibly limited the large number of victims.[14]

A responsible innovation governing body would aim at setting out the issues at stake in terms of the benefits for one or the other of the parties involved. This is particularly the case for patents, intellectual property which make up a significant part of responsible innovation. For instance, the company Myriad Genetics filed a patent for two genes which predisposed women to breast cancer. While these patents included entire exclusivity for all screening tests of these genes, the Institut Curie in France had in parallel developed a more reliable and less expensive screening method. Although the first patents were eventually ruled invalid, the question of responsibility is a related party to scientific discoveries of private laboratories and a responsible innovation governing body is the only way to anticipate these difficulties. Another example in a different sector would be the case of genetically modified organisms (GMO). Often criticized in France, they were originally developed to offer a considerable advantage: grow a wide variety of food in areas of the world with complex climate and environmental conditions. There is no doubt that this type of innovation represents a major advantage for populations affected by the great famines for instance. Still, two problems emerge: firstly, the question of potential risks remains unsettled. What are the risks in the medium and long term of the use and consumption of genetically-modified products? Secondly, and perhaps more importantly, the use of GMOs is not typically implemented where it would be the most relevant. Indeed, GMOs are very widely used on lands that do not actually present any difficulty for growing crops. The challenge then lies uniquely in increasing the crop yield of these very lands. We can, therefore, see a diversion from the use of what could potentially be a responsible innovation to one which essentially is centered on increasing profit.

---

[14]Pavie, X (2012). *Innovation-responsable: Stratégie et levier de croissance des organisations*, p. 119. *Op. cit.*

Whether in the case of asbestos, where its harmfulness was discovered through usage, in the case of GMOs, where the misuse was openly recognized or in the case of patent protection, the importance of governance for implementing responsible innovation becomes clear. The issue at stake for such governance would be, on the one hand, to maintain a certain tension between the innovation which is in circulation on the market and the continuous progress in scientific knowledge and that should be brought to the attention of users in terms of consequences. On the other hand, it would ensure that a particular innovation would indeed be aimed at benefitting society as a whole rather than a fraction of citizens.

This point regarding governance highlights the very much political aspect of responsible innovation. This aspect raises a question which concerns society, issued by and with citizens and for their sake.

This system of governance should be based on five principles[15]:

1. The common good: Does the innovation place the community at risk?
2. The public, the users must take part in the decision-making process: Have the users got the means needed to understand and decide?
3. Research and results must be published: Is the progress and evolution of knowledge being shared by and with all?
4. Impacts must be measured independently: Who owns the knowledge? In other words, we should aim at achieving a type of governance which is not attached to any financial interest concerning stakeholders; and
5. The setting up of governing bodies should precede the launch of innovations: Is every innovation project — which is considered to be potentially "at risk" — being correctly launched in terms of a surrounding and appropriate system of monitoring and governance?

These five principles help to guarantee a responsible innovation, without stifling the innovation element. The questions are used as a way of anticipating as much as possible the potential risks which may be linked to an innovation once it is launched. The challenge lies in successfully combining the time factor which is critical for competitiveness and the diffusion factor. A permanent and consistent monitoring system which systematically puts into question the potential risks is the only way to minimize negative impacts of innovations considered to be posing a risk.

---

[15] *Ibid.*, p. 120.

8. Responsibility Committees

The innovators are sometimes excluded from the final decision-making process which will determine whether or not to launch the innovation which they have been developing. This can cause them to lose their sense of ownership to the project they were initially working on. It is in this context that the responsible organization makes sense. As that there are numerous decision-making committees within organizations (Executive Committee, Sales Committee, Development Committee, Innovations Committee, etc.), we should perhaps consider where we could, within those very structures, integrate Responsibility Committees, whose purpose would be to measure, identify and observe the reaction of the organization at the place of impact of the innovation. While the implementation in itself is simple, the issues linked to it are particularly complex. This is, on the one hand, due to the difficulty of evaluating risks prior to market launch, but more importantly due to the necessity to take action as soon as risks arise depending on the hypotheses previously formulated. For instance, in the case of harmful waves which are potentially released by mobile phones, there clearly always was a doubt concerning the potential negative impacts on human health caused by these waves. This, however, does not mean that they should not have been launched, since the risk was not accurately proven, while impact studies were underway. Nevertheless, the mobile telephony operators could have partly assumed responsibility for the consequences of their product launch, by speculating on potential impacts by creating a series of hypotheses while awaiting results of brain tests:

- Hypothesis 1: Recall all mobile phones from the market;
- Hypothesis 2: Create a phone with no health risks (by providing a hands-free mobile phone kit, directly connected to the phone);
- Hypothesis 3: Mass communication operation providing clear information to customers regarding risks incurred.

It goes without saying that these hypotheses do not represent a particular obstacle in dealing with the intensity of market competition. When it comes to pricing agreements, operators sometimes know how to find areas of arrangement.

The role of Responsible Innovation Committees within organizations would thus be on the one hand to speculate and create a series of hypotheses linked to the potential risks surrounding the innovation. On the other hand, they would have the authority to put these hypotheses into practice if needed with the inherent economic constraints, depending on results obtained.

These committees would actually benefit most from operating as part of an inter-company network, enabling to share and agree on certain fundamental research and commonly decide on the actions required following the release of findings. In the case of mobile phones for instance, the establishment of a joint responsibility committee which decided to include a hands-free mobile phone kit would reduce the risk of being overtaken by a competitor on that point.[16]

9. Involving Citizens

An innovation does not become responsible solely through the responsible behavior of scientists and innovators; it also requires the participation of a broad segment of the public.

As a governance system is set up to face the uncertainty in a context of transparency, traceability, communication and iteration between the innovator and the possible discoveries to come, it is absolutely fundamental for the final user, who will be directly or indirectly impacted, to become a major actor at the heart of the debate. Responsibility is both individual and shared in society as it is in the organization. The Responsible Innovation Committees should become the most popular and privileged divisions within the firm, as they are the places where both value is created for the organization and the interests of individuals are preserved.

In the United Kingdom, for instance, *Research Councils* have developed an initiative to involve the public into their research by creating an environment whereby researchers themselves present their work to the public to get their feedback and opinion. In this way, the *Public Engagement in Science* ensures that members of the public are involved in the governance regarding choices made in relation to innovations which are considered to be posing a risk.

In France, the *OPECST* (Parliamentary Office for Evaluating Scientific and Technological Choices), aims at informing the Parliament of the consequences of certain scientific and technological choices in order to clarify

---

[16]Pavie, X (2012). *Innovation-responsable: Stratégie et levier de croissance des organisations*, p. 122. *Op. cit.*

the decision-making. A further task is to inform citizens, especially younger members, as was done through the program *"L'innovation face aux peurs et aux risques"* (Innovation in the face of fears and risks).[17]

Another example from France would be the *Grenelle de l'environment*[18] (Grenelle Environment Forum) I and II which was essentially an action process implemented in collaboration with various actors from different sectors of civil society to address environmental issues. In 1997, the CNDP (French national public debate commission) was created with the aim of fostering a more participative democracy. One of the major debates managed by this commission was the one which took place between October 15, 2009 and February 24, 2010 on nanotechnologies. The aim of the debate was to get stakeholders as a whole involved in addressing the surrounding issues such as the development of such technologies, regulations, danger and risk assessment procedures, etc. Unfortunately, the initiative did not turn out to be a major success, far from it. Indeed, committed lobbyists were the only few members who took part in these debates; regular citizens were very poorly represented in the end.

10.   The Case of the Nanocode

Responsible innovation is often addressed in the context of nanotechnologies and nanosciences. These are the study, manufacture and manipulation of structures, devices and hardware systems at the scale of less than 40 nanometers and combine various scientific disciplines: electronics, mechanics, chemistry, optics, biology, etc.

There are multiple applications for this type of science; in cosmetic products for instance, nanotechnologies are widely used in the form of nanoparticles. Certain active substances are encapsulated into these nanoparticles to give them new assets for improved effectiveness. This is the case for titanium dioxide nanoparticles used in sunscreen lotion to avoid the whitening of the skin. The idea is to encapsulate vitamins E which are then able

---

[17]Available at http://www.senat.fr/opecst/.

[18]The Grenelle de l'environnement is an open multi-party organization which hosts roundtable discussions and debates on a specific environment-related theme and brings together representatives from the government, local authorities, trade unions, business and voluntary sectors aiming at drawing up a plan of action for tackling environmental issues.

to penetrate through the skin. However, is this invasion through the skin really that harmless to human health when so little studies have been conducted on that topic? In fact, American research has pointed to the possible dangers of nanoparticles which are present in sunscreen lotions for the respiratory tracts, where the consequences could be comparable to those caused by asbestos. We should also extend this concern to researchers and technicians working in this sector as they may be at risk in their very workplace, without any certainty regarding the effectiveness of their protection gear.

It is partly for that reason, that governing bodies, codes and legislations among others, should be developed to address the new risks posed by these applications. In this context, the Royal Society (academy for Science in Great Britain), launched the Nanocode.[19]

In November 2006, the *Royal Society* alongside *Insight Investment* and the *Nanotechnology Industries Association* undertook a joint project exploring the economic and social impacts of technical, social and economic uncertainties linked to nanotechnologies. This collaboration led to the organization of a workshop aimed at stimulating companies to take into account the many questions linked to the development of nanotechnologies. This initiative gathered a group of 17 companies from around Europe, all sharing a common commercial interest for the sector of nanotechnologies, ranging from the food and drinks or the pharmaceuticals industries to the distribution of health products or fashion accessories. One of the main results was the unanimous agreement on the need for a voluntary code of practice for organizations involved with nanotechnologies. The consensus was that such a code of practice would be based on principles rather than standards; it would be developed in collaboration with representatives from business, including BASF, Unilever and Smith & Nephew as well as non-governmental organizations, consumer groups, trade unions and groups representing the government.

The purpose of the proposal for a code of practice, entitled *Responsible NanoCode*[20] was to establish an international consensus on best practice and provide support to organizations and firms by showing them methods of proving their internal responsible practices in the management of nanotechnologies, while awaiting potential complementary regulations to be put in place. The aim of this voluntary code of practice would be to

---

[19] Available at http://royalsociety.org/Responsible-NanoCode-for-business-to-be-developed/, http://www.responsiblenanocode.org/.
[20] Available at www.nanocode.eu.

ensure that nanotechnologies will reach their potential and provide benefits in terms of health, the environment, the society and the economy, at a time when companies are also facing technical, social, regulatory and commercial uncertainties regarding these relatively new technologies. The code of practice outlines that organizations should follow seven principles as follows:

1. Ensure that the organization's board of directors or its leadership body is responsible for managing its involvement with nanotechnologies;
2. Initiate a dialogue with actors of the nanotechnology industry and be responsive to their views with regards the development or use of products which contain nanotechnologies;
3. Identify and minimize sources of risk for employees handling products containing nanotechnologies, at every stage of the production process or during industrial use, in order to ensure high standards of safety and health in the workplace;
4. Conduct a thorough evaluation of risks and minimize all potential risks to public health, safety and the environment linked to products containing nanotechnologies;
5. Take into account and react to all involvement and all social or ethical impacts resulting from the development or commercialization of products containing nanotechnologies;
6. Adopt responsible practices for the commercialization and marketing of products containing nanotechnologies; and
7. Initiate a dialogue with suppliers and/or commercial partners to encourage and stimulate their adoption of the code of practice and in this way ensure their ability to fulfill the commitments they have made in that regard.

11. Case Studies

a. *Veja*

Veja was established in 2004 with a vision of developing a responsible and sustainable fashion brand. The company aims to achieve high social and environmental standards — actively promoting eco-farming, campaigning against deforestation, supporting workers' rights and creating employment for poor families. Veja's ethics have earned third party endorsement from the IBD accreditation scheme which works across South America to encourage humanistic principles and the preservation of the environment.

The company's holistic approach touches every part of its supply chain — including transportation, packaging and head office carbon emissions. Following are some of the steps they have taken in this direction:

- Veja sources cotton and rubber from co-operative cotton growers and rubber tappers. Despite paying between 30% and 100% above the world market price for its raw materials.
- The cotton used by Veja is harvested by an association of small farmers located in one of Brazil's poorest areas, Ceará. Veja workers grow their food as well as cotton for the project under agro-ecology principles, which ban the use of chemicals and pesticides.
- Veja buys rubber from tappers in Amazon at a premium, providing producer returns that remove the temptation for tappers to supplement their incomes through land clearing, cattle breeding or wood extraction. This, in turn, helps protect large areas of forest and conserve local biodiversity.
- It also works with communities to introduce to the region a non-industrial new technology: Folha Desfumada Liquida (FDL). FDL allows rubbers tappers to process freshly harvested rubber into a semi-finished product.
- Shoe assembly takes place at a factory in Vale dos Sinos, South Brazil, where workers enjoy dignified conditions, employment rights and fair pay for overtime.
- When the goods arrive in France — having been transported by ship — they are stored and dispatched by Ateliers Sans Frontières, a French social charity that helps the disadvantaged reintegrate into society through work.
- Shoe boxes are made of recycled and recyclable cardboard, while the company powers its headquarters with renewable energy supplied by Enercoop.
- Leather used for the shoe collections is tanned with acacia extracts, a natural, non-polluting alternative to metals, such as chrome.

b. *Arup*

Arup launched an initiative to increase the number of SMEs in its supply chain and support their sustainable development. It helped the company save roughly £1.1 million last year and reduce waste, energy consumption and travel costs.

To increase its supply base of SMEs, Arup established development plans in each of its main purchasing categories recruitment services, travel, facilities and outside consultancies. These were supported by sustainable development actions like free administrative support during the start up phase, volume commitments to help partners grow, workshops to find joint savings opportunities and free consultancy to help partners develop their own sustainability plans.

As a result Arup now works with 25% more SMEs, and all suppliers are signed up to its Sustainable Procurement Plan. The project has notched up several achievements, with providers joining carbon retirement programs and committing to respect all labor laws and human rights legislation. Meanwhile, Arup developed the British standard for sustainable event management, producing 15% less carbon in the process.

c. Lend Lease

Lend Lease has taken several initiatives to improve the sustainability of its own procurement process and the performance of its supply chain. These changes have resulted in the company creating industry-wide change around the responsible sourcing of construction materials.

Lend Lease developed "Building Confidence," an accreditation scheme for the construction industry with the help of Achilles. It audits providers on key issues like quality, health and safety, environmental, social and ethical performance. It is now used by 16% peer-buying organizations. To monitor onsite performance Lend Lease created Supply Chain Solutions, monitoring suppliers every four months to ensure they continue to meet its high standards. The company was also the first major UK construction contractor to achieve FSC Project certification for its procurement practice.

The company's interventions so far have led to the increased availability of responsibly sourced materials.

d. PepsiCo

PepsiCo UK is investing in tools and techniques to cut the water use and carbon emissions involved in farming potatoes, oats and apples for its products by 50% in five years.

PepsiCo's will, by 2015, replace 75% of crops with higher-yield varieties that are more disease-resistant and less dependent on water and fertilizer. The company is investing in drip irrigation and working with suppliers to champion low-carbon alternative fertilizers.

In 2011, 70 of PepsiCo's British farm suppliers had adopted "i-crop" and "cool farm" technologies to help fight climate change. The tools accurately calculate soil moisture and carbon emissions to give farmers a better understanding of how and when to fertilize and irrigate efficiently.

Growers achieved a 7% reduction in carbon output and a 10% drop in water use in the project's first year. Crops required 18% less fertilizer and the company started to roll out a new potato variety, promising 17% more yield with 33% less water.

e. *Skanska, UK*

Skanska, UK, an international project development and construction company, aims to build deep green buildings and infrastructure all with a near-zero impact on the environment. To achieve this ambitious vision, it needs to work closely with its supply chain.

Over the past two years Skanska, UK has reviewed, modified and in some cases, overhauled the way the company procures products and services to set itself firmly on the road to sustainability. Supply chain forums and supplier relationship meetings have been extensively used, along with a sustainability procurement champion.

Skanska now gives preference to using suppliers who have signed up to its sustainable procurement principles. High-risk trades undergo a two-day intensive audit to establish levels of compliance with its procurement policies. An outcome of the audit is a detailed report which drives the joint development of an action plan for any issues identified. In just one year, the number of non-compliance cases has been cut by a third.

The company defines sustainable procurement around six key areas: supply chain health and safety; ethical sourcing; supply chain equality, diversity and inclusion; environmental and green sourcing and, finally, best value procurement and supply chain quality management.

The company has secured funding from Construction Skills to launch a Sustainable Supply Chain School, an interactive web portal that will help suppliers develop their sustainability knowledge and skills.

f. *Marks & Spencer (M&S)*

Marks & Spencer's (M&S) sustainability vision involves being a fair retail partner and setting transformative ethical and environmental standards essential to the future of the business. Its initiatives cover a range of challenges in its global supply chain, which M&S reckons to accounts for about 80% of its footprint.

Plan A: Launched in 2007, Plan A, M&S's sustainability program lists 180 commitments to address the retailer's most material impacts. In 2010/11 alone, it delivered £70 million in net benefits, which M&S will plough back into its sustainability work. The company has improved energy efficiency (25%), cut waste (34%), addressed the sustainability of raw materials, developed healthy product ranges and taken its work on ethical trade to a new level. Plan A has seen a fundamental change in how M&S does business with suppliers, backed by an extensive audit scheme — earning the company its place as a consistently highly-rated organization in the Ethical Trading Initiative. The supply chain agenda is championed by senior leaders and backed by financial incentives for the M&S buying teams, as well as a £50 million fund providing capital for suppliers to introduce new ways of working.

The most immediate major target is to have a sustainability credential attached to 50% of products by 2015. Some projects underway involving suppliers, NGO partners and respected experts. Among them are: a move to 100% sustainable timber, fish and palm oil; introduction of living wages at 15 overseas factories; sustainable cotton sourcing; engaging dozens of farmers in a sustainable agriculture project; green factory programs; an eco-dyehouse initiative; and packaging reduction and recycling partnerships. On the fair trade front, M&S is pursuing its ethical framework, a Factory Ethical Excellence initiative and a program to train 500,000 supply chain workers in their rights, as well as support for disadvantaged workers and producers. On the environmental front, M&S helps suppliers reduce dependency on fossil fuels and vulnerable ecosystems, protecting biodiversity and the environmental rights of local communities. It also has policies for the sustainable sourcing of cotton, wood, palm oil, soy, fish, leather, beef, cocoa and coffee.

Success stories include individual achievements like zero waste to landfill, 50% reduction in water use, 290 tons of waste savings, 30% less energy use, 10% reductions in staff turnover, fewer accidents and salary increases of up to 50%. To date, 250 food suppliers have adopted the ethical and environmental guidance; 1,380 clothing factories are compliant with M&S's environmental and chemical policies and 25% of products have sustainability elements. Indeed, 76% of the wood used in products, 90% of fish and the palm oil in 329 products are now sourced in a sustainable way. Supplier partnerships have also led to product innovation, including carbon neutral bras, fleeces made from recycled polyester and a cashmere coat made from returned jumpers.

CONCLUSION

There is an obvious contradiction between one's concern to act responsibly, thereby anticipating and calculating potential impacts of an innovation and the need to let unbridled creativity run freely, to step beyond existing frameworks, to think of the impossible. In his book "The Wisdom of the Physicist,"[1] Yves Quéré claims that the physicist is, above all, an unreasonable human being. In the same way that it is necessary to be *insane* for believing that a seemingly solid material actually consists of void and moving atoms, a similar unreasonable state of mind is required to explore the boundaries of what is possible and to go down the road of the unknown, leading to true innovations. However, the need to be unreasonable to innovate in this way does not absolve the innovator of all responsibility in relation to the consequences of his or her actions. It is therefore up to the innovator, to apply the criteria of responsible choices and decisions as he or she is progressing through the path of uncertainty, that is, the innovation setting. Therefore, one can only progress if discovery is determined by the curiosity and exploration of the extreme unknown. The innovation which actually results from such discovery however, is constrained by ethics.

What kind of a process will ensure that the innovation will push back the boundaries of possibility and cross new frontiers while being wholly responsible? The case studies presented in this work are proof that implementing a responsible innovation strategy correctly opens up new opportunities, effectively becoming a catalyst for creativity and providing major leverage to achieve innovation and performance within a responsible framework. Nevertheless, this integration process needs to be implemented correctly in order to deliver the required performance objectives.

---

[1] Quéré, Y (2006). *La sagesse du physicien.* Paris: L'œil neuf editions.

Responsible innovation can be partly described as a wicked problem,[2] defined by the difficulty, perhaps even the impossibility to provide a clear, complete and non-contradictory answer to the questions it raises. Moreover, wicked problems are characterized by constant change. This very nature of problem entirely applies to responsible innovation, in the sense that innovation allows therapeutic cloning thereby risking human cloning or where nuclear power provides energy as much as the possibility of mass destruction or even where genetically modified organisms (GMOs) can provide as much access to mass food supplies as they can lead to over-exploitation, the list goes on. What is the best way to deal with innovation that can bring so many positive elements but whose negative effects can equate the former, in some cases even outdo them? Laws, legislation, ethical treaties, charters, etc. can certainly make up part of a better control system. However, the globalized and increasingly globalizing world we are living in makes it ever more complicated to monitor the correct application of rules. This complexity is increased by the variations in understanding of these rules and their applications according to different cultures.

How can this problem be resolved? The answer is threefold.

The first point is that this problem cannot be resolved by one person alone. Innovation creates choices and can give rise to new lifestyles — these choices cannot be kept by innovators and scientists, but need to be shared by all citizens. The role of innovators is indeed to contribute positively to progress in order to improve the well-being of individuals. However, the latter must, more so than ever, be involved in the research, applications and issues being generated as a result. This may come at a cost, perhaps in terms of an extension of the time needed to deploy the project,[3] certainly in terms of brakes to certain aspects linked to the project, presumably in terms of rejection of certain surrounding factors. However, it will come to the benefit of a much needed common agreement regarding the path that scientific research and progress must take, as it now addresses human values. Whether it concerns the transgression of these very values, the distortion of their context regarding genetics or the environment, today's innovators cannot form part of a coterie, confiscating the fundamental issues regarding the future of mankind from the rest of the world — the issues at stake are now of too great importance.

---

[2]Churchman, CW (1967). Guest editorial. *Management Science*, 14(4).
[3]See the call launched for a "slowscience." Available at http://slowscience.fr/.

The other two points concern the innovators themselves, who constantly re-design our everyday lives. The products and services surrounding us essentially trigger changes which impact on our lifestyles. Whether in the case of a social network or a mobile phone, we have seen that the various impacts on health, safety or the environment cannot be under-estimated. The innovators within their organizational structures are not like any other employee, as they bear responsibility for the world of tomorrow, no matter how insignificant their innovations may seem at the time. This responsibility must be recognized by the person who takes on that role, as well as the person appointing that individual. While the role of the innovator generates few rights, it includes many duties. That person, therefore, needs to understand and embrace the multi-faceted nature of the role. Through their understanding of society and of their innovation with its potential risks and impacts, the innovator becomes the sole individual capable of creating a set of hypotheses with regards to these risks which will be tested once the project is launched.

The first and perhaps most important duty of the innovator also comes as the third fact: the innovator must care for others, thereby, introducing the notion of innovation-care as a key concept within responsible innovation. Managers and innovators should make up part of the official "deliverers" of care, since their decisions will ultimately impact directly or indirectly various members of society. While kindness and care for others are key notions within the concept of innovation-care, it must be underlined that the notion of "care" is nevertheless subordinate to the actual "innovation" component. In other terms, while the *innovator-carers* are defined by their ability to stop an innovation, their first objective is to achieve economic performance. Care is therefore not a frame nor is it a brake to innovation, but should rather become a process which can be articulated to and with it. It can never replace the ultimate goal of innovation, since the latter is measured in terms of the performance, growth, sustainability of the organization and the improvement of the individual's life. As innovation-care is only at the beginning of its existence, it remains to be integrated in practice into economic models. In the same idea behind the responsible innovation concept, it requires the entire commitment of the organization.

Society as a whole needs to be entirely involved in the monitoring, verifying and ultimate decision process regarding the acceptance of an innovation. As the innovator is required to care for members of society around him, so are those very members required to be fully part of the process which may, if not determine, at least play a critical role in the future development of society. It is however the innovator's duty to perform that first transformation. The opinions of individuals are not required for all innovations, as these will not be able to fully comprehend the in's and out's of every innovation project. The innovator should therefore accept a sort of moral duty towards society and its human values as well as an ethical engagement towards citizens. For this reason, the issue at stake within responsible innovation is primarily of a political nature whereby society as a whole is concerned, with a citizen who is as much an actor as a beneficiary.

Ancient philosophy consists of "spiritual exercises,"[4] meaning any practice intended to transform, in them or in others, the way of life, or the outlook on the latter. It is both an internal and external dialogue as well as a practical implementation. Ancient philosophy is therefore a discipline destined to help human beings to live better with what they have rather than live from their unsatisfied passions, such as glory, money, success and possessions. Through various exercises including meditation, asceticism, writing, reading, dialogue, etc., the individual no longer acts without thinking but rather becomes accustomed to acting within a conditioned framework aimed at being better and living better. While practicing such spiritual exercises used to be part of the daily occupations of ancient thinkers such as Epicurus, Diogenes and Epictetus, they are nonetheless part of contemporary philosophy: Emerson, Thoreau and Foucault were also practitioners of such exercises. Ancient spiritual exercises can therefore be considered as a way of experimenting for innovators who struggle with existential questions regarding the "right" or "wrong" choice for launching an innovation in society.[5] May these last few lines not be considered conclusive, but rather be understood as a further commitment towards establishing the philosophical basis for responsible innovation.

---

[4]Hadot, P (2001). *La philosophie comme manière de vivre*, p. 149. Paris: Albin Michel.
[5]Pavie, X (2009). *L'apprentissage de soi*. Paris: Eyrolles; Pavie, X (2010). *La meditation philosophique*. Paris: Eyrolles.

APPENDIX

Case Study: Starbucks

Despite being often caricatured as the equivalent of McDonald's in the coffee industry by causing the disappearance of small local bistros and cafés, Starbucks' offer has always differed widely from its competitors since its creation in 1971. Indeed, the world's current leading coffee chain offers its customers a whole experience surrounding coffee that combines a friendly coffee shop atmosphere with an active willingness to educate its customers and encourage them to achieve a responsible mode of consumption.

The first Starbucks opened its doors approximately forty years ago, under the name of a character from Herman Melville's novel: *"Moby Dick."* Referring to the romantic aspect of the seaside and maritime tradition, Starbucks' founder believed that the name reflected perfectly the carefully selected coffee products of excellent quality, as well as the import activities of the best coffees in the world made exclusively available for Seattle coffee amateurs.

Howard Schultz began working for Starbucks in 1982. During a trip to Italy, he discovered the fascinating Italian-style espresso bars and with it the wonderfully unique experience surrounding it, where people take time to talk over a cup of coffee. In 1984, Schultz decided to open his very first own coffee shop in the United States, inspired from the warm and welcoming Italian style, where customers can read newspapers and enjoy salads, sandwiches and coffee, all sharing the Starbucks logo. Three years later, Schultz buys Starbucks from his previous employers and starts building his own success story, starting in the United States and later expanding into the rest of the world. Today, Starbucks represents over 16,000 stores across 50 countries around the world, providing more than 45 million customers per week its famous coffee supplied directly from its five roasting plants.

A unique customer experience

Starbucks' ambition never consisted in competing with small local bistros. Rather, it aims to provide a new consumer experience: a welcoming place where all generations can either simply drop by for a take away order or sit in comfortably for a few hours to talk, work, relax, connect to the Internet, discover new music and so on. The Starbucks experience is about being elsewhere, but in the comfort of a place that feels "just like home," feeling safe and welcome, close to people who share similar values. Rather than focusing on adapting to different cultures and traditions, Starbucks has built its success and development for the past 30 years by concentrating on the consumer as an individual with universal needs.

Howard Schulz considers the idea of serving coffee as one of the most common human needs on the planet. Starbucks aims to meet universal needs, instead of focusing on those of specific nationalities. While the quality of Starbucks products is of rational importance to the company, its first goal is to create an emotional connection with its customers. Coca Cola does not simply sell sweet water, in the same way that Nike does not only sell running shoes or even Apple does not just sell computers. Starbucks similarly strives beyond its coffee to sell emotion all over the world, regardless of its customers' origins, by providing a 'third place,' situated between the workplace and the home. The welcoming feeling which defines this 'new place' is part of the reason for the higher rates of women (70%) and young workers customers, who previously did not go to local bistros.

The success of offering this new welcoming place largely depends on the commitment of staff to actively strive toward this shared goal, which in turn depends on Starbucks management's ability to make their coffee shops an 'ideal' place to work in to ensure service quality remains at the highest level. Each and every employee must therefore share Starbucks' own values which include being recognized as much for its environmental and community programs as it is for the quality of its coffee. They have translated this into a responsible policy which consists of three organizational axes: ethical purchasing, community involvement and environmental responsibility.

Purchasing, production and consumption places

At Starbucks, ethical purchasing is defined as a commitment to solely purchase a high-quality Arabica coffee which is grown responsibly and part of ethical commercial practices. As well as controlling the environmental impact from its production process, Starbucks is committed to take care of its coffee suppliers, as they are intimately linked to added value for Starbucks. Since 2010, all espressos, caffès latte and cappuccinos are stamped Max Havelaar, certifying Starbuck's commitment.

Starbucks' coffee suppliers vary by their size and economic structures, meaning there is a mixture of small producers, cooperatives as well as more industrialized suppliers. It is important to note that Starbucks' business approach with small producers is a guarantee of the quality of their produce as well as quantity and sustainability.

In 1998, a protocol is signed between the Conservation International association and Starbucks for a pilot program in coffee supply. Founded in 1987, Conservation International's mission includes protecting and preserving the planet's natural heritage and global biodiversity while showing how human societies can live in harmony with nature. Its goal is to build alliances with companies, conservation groups, governments and private structures. In the middle of the 1990s, Conservation International identified coffee as an important element capable of affecting biodiversity and environmental preservation. As coffee is grown in full sun and involves the use of agrochemical products, it can have a devastating effect on the environment. In consequence, at the end of the 1990s, Conservation International launched a project in collaboration with three coffee cooperatives in Chiapas (Mexico) in order to preserve and promote coffee grown in the shade. The region was home to a large number of rare and endangered bird species. The program aimed to preserve and promote coffee grown in the shade and prevent deforestation in that region.

As part of the project, Starbucks undertook a communication initiative to Mexican farmers in order to inform them about the technical changes needed for growing a high-quality coffee in the shade. At the time, Starbucks did not buy these farmers' produce but it was agreed that they would do so at a preferential price, if the coffee met Starbucks' quality standards. Within the first year of the project, Starbucks bought 76,000 pounds of 'shade-grown' coffee from the Chiapas farms at a higher price than that on the market (an average of $1.20 per pound in 2001). The Chiapas project generated a 40% increase in farmers' revenue, while international coffee sales from partner cooperatives grew by 100%.

Starbucks actively supported the non-profitable organization that is Conservation International by providing training to farmers, cooperative managers, and technical staff in terms of quality management control and environmentally-friendly agricultural methods. This successful alliance innovation proved to benefit both Starbucks management and customers. At the same time, Conservation International and small coffee producers had the opportunity to develop their skills and profits while also preserving the environment.

Starbucks' commitment and implementation programs towards its producers are continuously verified by 160 independent accredited inspectors and supervised by the Scientific Certification Systems, an independent environmental organism that controls the sustainable and quality aspects of ingredients: certification, audit, test and standard. In 2008, 77% of the coffee distributed by Starbucks was in line with these standards. The company aims to extend this to all of its stores by 2015. Starbucks' efforts for involving independent farmers into production processes, for being a part of various communities and their environment made it the most powerful buyer of Fair trade certified coffee in the world in 2009. The goal is to collectively produce a coffee that still meets excellent quality standards while taking care of the whole ecosystem, by also developing financing programs for allocating budgetary provisions if needed. Thanks to this initiative, the Costa Rican and African centers are forecast to invest in programs worth over $20 million by 2015.

A global approach

Responsibility towards suppliers only makes sense within a structure of global responsible actions where the entire value chain is taken into account, since a reduction in environmental footprint can only be measured as a whole. For this reason, the consumption of energy resources such as water and electricity is closely monitored in Starbucks restaurants, whether it is for washing dishes, general cleaning, in-store climate control, etc. They even go as far as monitoring their cups, which Starbucks aim to guarantee 100% recycled and recyclable.

Each new store opened over the last few years, aims to conform to the LEED® (Leadership in Energy and Environmental Design) certification. The latter was developed in 1994 by the US Green Building Council — an American association dedicated to the promotion of profitable buildings, comfortable to live in and which guaranteed an efficient environmental performance.

Employees are key within this responsible value chain. From the moment he took over, Schultz's main concern was to grow his employee's loyalty. He believes that Starbucks' aura must ultimately go beyond its coffee, its restaurants, even its employees. Its role must be more global and its employees must, for this reason, be involved in the communities in which they operate. This involvement can range from providing educational support at local schools, help for the disabled or disadvantaged members of the community, etc. Starbucks employees contribute one million hours per year to such activities.

BIBLIOGRAPHY

Acquier, A, Gond, J-P and Igalens, J (2011). *La religion dans les affaires: la RSE (Responsabilité sociale de l'entreprise)*. Fondapol (May 2011).

Alleman, JE and Brooke, TM (1997). Asbestos Revisited. *Scientific American*, July, 70–75.

Balaudé, JF (2010). *Le savoir-vivre philosophique. Empédocle, Socrate et Platon*. Paris: Grasset.

Barnard, CI (1938). *The Functions of the Executive*. Cambridge, MA: Harvard University Press.

Bensaude-Vincent, B (2009). *Colloque innovation-responsable*. Collège de France, April.

Bentham, J and Bozovic, M (1995). *The Panopticon Writings*, pp. 29–95. London: Verso.

Black, E (2001). *IBM and Holocaust: The Strategic Alliance between Nazi Germany and America's Most Powerful Corporation*. London: Little Brown.

Botterhuis, L, van der Duin, P, de Ruijter, P and van Wijck, P (2010). Monitoring the future. Building an early warning system for the Dutch Ministry of Justice. *Futures*, 42, 454–465.

Brundtland, GH (1987). Report of the World Commission on Environment and Development: Our Common Future. New York: United Nations General Assembly.

Butner, K (2011). Driving performance through sustainability: Strategy, synergy and significance. Executive report, *IBM Global Business Services*. (Online). Available at ftp://public.dhe.ibm.com/common/ssi/ecm/en/gbe03414usen/GBE03414USEN.PDF. Accessed on March 13, 2013.

Caroll, AB (1979). A three-dimensional conceptual model of corporate social performance. *Academy of Management Review*, 4, 497–505.

Caroll, AB (1994). Social issues in management research: Expert's views, analysis and commentary. *Business & Society*, 33, 5–29.

Caroll, AB (1999). Corporate social responsibility. *Business & Society*, 38(3), 268–295.

Carson, R (1962). *Silent Spring*. Boston: Houghton Mifflin Harcourt.

Chesbrough, HW (2003). The era of open innovation. *MIT Sloan Management Review*, 44(3), 34–41.

Christensen, CM (1997). *The Innovator's Dilemma. When New Technologies Cause Great Firms to Fail*. Harvard Business School Press.

Churchman, CW (1967). Guest editorial. *Management Science*, 14(4).

Clark, JM (1939). *Social Control of Business*, 2nd Edition. New York: McGraw-Hill.

CNW Marketing Research Inc. (2007). Dust to Dust: The Energy Cost of New Vehicles From Concept to Disposal.

Cohen, WM and Levinthal, DA (1990). Absorptive capacity: A new perspective on learning and innovation. *Administrative Science Quarterly*, 35(1), 128–152.

Collingridge, D (1980). *The Social Control of Technology*. New York: St. Martin's Press; London: Pinter.

Dahlander, L and Frederiksen, L (2012). The core and cosmopolitans: A relational view of innovation in user communities. *Organization Science*, 23(4), 988–1007.

De Sadeleer, N (2011). *Le Principe de précaution dans le monde*. Paris: Fondapol.

Dickson, PR and Giglierano, JJ (1986). Missing the boat and sinking the boat: A conceptual model of entrepreneurial risk. *Journal of Marketing*, 50, 58–70.

Donaldson, T and Preston, LE (1995). The stakeholder theory of the corporation: Concepts, evidence and implications. *The Academy of Management Review*, 20(1), 65–91.

Dubigeon, O (2009). *Piloter un développement responsable. Quels processus pour l'entreprise?* 3e Edition. Paris: Pearson Education.

Eccles, RG and Serafeim, G (2013). The performance frontier: Innovating for a sustainable strategy. *Harvard Business Review*, 91(5), 50–60.

Elkington, J (1997). *Cannibals with Forks, the Triple Bottom Lines of the 21st Century Business*. Oxford: Capstone Publishing.

Engel, L (1997). Réguler les comportements. In Ferenczi, T (Ed.), *De quoi sommes-nous responsables?*, pp. 11–36; 80–89. Editions Le Monde.

Ernult, J and Ashta, A (2007). Développement durable, responsabilité société de l'entreprise, théroei des parties prenantes: Evolution et perspectives. *Cahiers du CEREN*, 21, 4–31.

Etzkowitz, H (2008). *The Triple Helix: University–Industry–Government Innovation in Action*. London: Routledge.

Ewald, F (1996). *Histoire de l'Etat-Providence*, p. 86. Paris: LGF.

Falk, R (2007). Measuring the effects of public support schemes on firms' innovation activities. Survey evidence from Austria. *Research Policy*, 36(5), 665–679.

Foucault, M (2001). *Usage des plaisirs et techniques de soi*. Reprinted in *Dits et Ecrits II*, p. 1358. Paris: Gallimard.

Fransman, M (1990). *The Market and Beyond: Cooperation and Competition in Information Technology Development in the Japanese System*. Cambridge: Cambridge University Press.

Freelancers Union (2013). Homepage. (Online). Available at www.freelancersunion.org. (accessed on March 13, 2013).

Freeman, RE (1984). *Strategic Management: A Stakeholder Approach*, p. 48. Boston: Piman-Ballinger.

Friedmann, G (1970). *La puissance et la sagesse*, p. 55. Paris: Gallimard.

Gagnepain, L (2006). La climatisation automobile — Impacts consommation et pollution. In *Repères*. Agency for Environment and Energy Management, Department of Transport Technology.

Gargiulo, M and Benassi, M (2000). Trapped in your own net? Network cohesion, structural holes, and the adaptation of social capital. *Organizational Science*, 11, 183–196.

Georghiou, L *et al.* (2003). Raising EU R&D intensity: Improving the effectiveness of public support mechanisms for private sector research and development. *Direct Measures 2003*, EUR 20716.

Gleick, PH (2007). Hummer versus Prius. "Dust to Dust" report Misleads the Media and Public with Bad Science. *CNW Marketing*.

Gorgoni, G (2006). La responsabilité comme projet. In Eberhard, C (Ed.), *Traduire nos responsabilités planétaires. Recomposer nos paysages juridiques*, pp. 131–146. Bruxelles: Bruylant.

Greenwood, M (2007). Stakeholder engagement: Beyond the myth of corporate responsibility. *Journal of Business Ethics*, 74, 315–327.

Hadot, P (2001). *La philosophie comme manière de vivre*, p. 149. Paris: Albin Michel.

Henderson, R and Clark, K (1990). Architectural innovation. The reconfiguration of existing product technologies and the failure of established firms. *Administrative Science Quarterly*, 35(1), 81–112.

Igalens, J and Benraiss, L (2005). Aux fondements de l'audit social: Howard R. Bowen et les églises protestantes. Actes de la 23e Université d'été de l'Audit social, 1 et 2 septembre 2005, IAE de Lille. (In French.)

Jonas, H (1979). *Das Prinzip Verantwortung — Versuch einer Ethik für die technologische Zivilisation*. Frankfurt am Main: Suhrkamp. (In German.)

Jonas, H (1979). *Le Principe responsabilité. Une éthique pour la civilisation technologique*. Trad. Greisch, J (1998). Paris: Flammarion (PR).

Jonas, H (1984). *The Imperative of Responsibility: In Search of Ethics for the Technological Age.* Chicago: University of Chicago Press.

Kant, I (1965). *Logique* (Vrin), p. 25.

Kant, I (2006). *Fondation de la métaphysique des mœurs.* In Métaphysique des mœurs, trad. Alain Renaut, Paris: Flammarion, 97–108.

Kramer, M, Pfitzer, M and Lee, P (2005). Competitive social responsibility: Uncovering the economic rationale for corporate social responsibility among Danish small and medium-sized enterprises. Foundation Strategy Group & Center for Business and Government, John F. Kennedy School of Government, Harvard University. (Online.) Available at http://www.eogs.dk/sw26505.asp. Accessed on August 20, 2009.

Kreps, T (1940). Measurement of the social performance of business. *An Investigation of Concentration of Economic Power for the Temporary National Economic Committee* (Monograph No. 7). Washington, DC: US Government Printing Office.

Laugier, S and Paperman, P (2008). La voix différente et les éthiques du care. In Giligan, C (Ed.), *Une voix différente,* pp. III–XXIV. Paris: Flammarion.

Lenglet, R (1996). *L'Affaire de l'amiante.* Paris: La Découverte Enquêtes.

Le service public de l'accès au droit (2004). *Charte de l'environnement de 2004.* (Online.) Available at http://www.legifrance.gouv.fr/Droit-francais/Constitution/Charte-de-l-environnement-de-2004. Accessed on March 16, 2013.

Lopez-Perez, V, Perez-Lopez, C and Rodriguez-Ariza, L (2007). The opinion of European companies on corporate social responsibility and its relation to innovation. *Issues in Social and Environmental Accounting,* 1(2), 276–295.

MacGregor, SP and Fontrodona, J (2008). Exploring the fit between CSR and innovation. *Working Paper,* IESE CBS, Barcelona.

McWilliams, A, Siegel, DS and Wright, PM (2006). Guest editor's introduction. Corporate social responsibility: Strategic implications. *Journal of Management Studies,* 43(1), 1–18.

Milne, AA (1926). *Winnie-the-Pooh.* London: Methuen & Co. Ltd.

Moore, GA (1999). *Crossing the Chasm.* New York: Harper Collins Publishers.

Moore, GE (2008). *Principia Ethica.* Cambridge: Cambridge University Press.

Mullins, JW and Forlani, D (2005). Missing the boat or sinking the boat: A study of new venture decision making. *Journal of Business Venturing,* 20(1), 47–69.

Myers, S and Marquis, DG (1969). Successful industrial innovation: A study of factors underlying innovation in selected firms. *National Science Foundation, NSF 69-17.* In Trott, P (2005), *Innovation Management and New Product Development,* 3rd Edition, p. 15. Harlow: Prentice Hall.

Nidumolu, R, Prahalad, CK and Rangaswami, MR (2009). Why sustainability is now the key driver of innovation. *Harvard Business Review,* 57–64.

Owen, R, Macnaghten, P and Stilgoe, J (2012). Responsible research and innovation: From science in society to science for society, with society. *Science and Public Policy,* 39(6), 751–760.

Pavie, X (2009). *L'apprentissage de soi.* Paris: Eyrolles.

Pavie, X (2010). *La méditation philosophique.* Paris: Eyrolles.

Pavie, X (2011a). The importance of responsible-innovation and the necessity of innovation-care. Working Paper ESSEC 1203.

Pavie, X (2011b). De quoi l'innovation-responsable est-elle le nom? *Cahier Innovation & Society,* November.

Pavie, X (2011c). Innovation responsable: Oxymore ou réalité. *Cahier Innovation & Society,* June.

Pavie, X (2012). *Innovation-responsable: Stratégie et levier de croissance pour les organisations.* Paris: Eyrolles.

Pavie, X and Carthy, D (2012). A strategy and process for integrating responsible-innovation into organisations. Presented at the 2nd Conference on Responsible-Innovation (Maatschappelijk Verantwoord Innoveren), December 13–14, 2012.

Pavie, X and Carthy, D (2013). Responsible-innovation in practice: How to implement responsibility across an organization. *Cahier Innovation & Society,* No. 33.

Pedersen, ER (2010). Modelling CSR: How managers understand the responsibilities on business toward society. *Journal of Business Ethics,* 91(2), 155–166.

Pommier, E (2012). *Hans Jonas et le Principe Responsabilité.* Paris: Presses Universitaires de France.

Porter, M (1985). *Competitive Advantage: Creating and Sustaining Superior Performance.* New York: Free Press.

Porter, M (2003). CSR — A religion with too many priests? *European Business Forum. Interview with Mette Morsig.* (Online.) 15 (Autumn). Available at http://www.fsg.org/Portals/0/Uploads/Documents/PDF/ CSR_Religion_with_Too_Many_Priests.pdf?cpgn=WP % 20DL %20- % 20CSR % 20- % 20 A % 20 Religion % 20 With % 20 too % 20 Many %20 Priests. (accessed on March 13, 2013).

Quéré, Y (2006). *La sagesse du physicien.* Paris: L'œil neuf editions.

Raymond, J (2003). La Ford Pinto: le contre-exemple américain. *Le Polyscope Le journal de l'Ecole polytechnique de Montréal,* 36.

Rittel, HWJ and Webber, MM (1973). Dilemmas in a general theory of planning. *Policy Sciences*, 4, 155–169.

Pedersen, ER (2010). Modelling CSR: How managers understand the responsibilities on business toward society. *Journal of Business Ethics*, 155–166.

Simon, HA (1957). *Models of Man*. New York: Wiley & Sons.

Schilling, MA (2005). A "Small-World" network model of cognitive insight. *Creativity Research Journal*, 17(2–3), 131–154.

Schot, J and Rip, A (1997). The past and future of constructive technology assessment. *Technological Forecasting & Social Change*, 54, 251–268.

Schumpeter, J (1912). *Economic Doctrine and Method: An Historical Sketch*. New York: Oxford University Press. Translated from German (1912) in 1954.

Schumpeter, J (1934). *The Theory of Economic Development*. Boston: Harvard University Press.

Schumpeter, J (1939). *Business Cycles: A Theoretical, Historical and Statistical Analysis of the Capitalist Process*, p. 105. New York: McGraw-Hill.

Schwartz, MS (2005). Universal moral values for corporate codes of ethics. *Journal of Business Ethics,* 59, 27–44.

Shaw, WH and Barry, V (1995). *Moral Issues in Business*, 6th Edition. Belmont: Wadsworth Publishing Company.

Shane, S (2002). Executive forum: University technology transfer to entrepreneurial companies. *Journal of Business Venturing*, 17, 537–552.

Stevenson, HH and Gumpert, D (1985). The heart of entrepreneurship. *Harvard Business Review*, 85, 85–94.

The HealthStore Foundation (2013). Homepage. (Online.) Available at www.cfwshops.org. Accessed on March 13, 2013.

Tortoriello, M and Krackhardt, D (2010). Activating cross-boundary knowledge: The role of Simmelian ties in the generation of innovations. *Academic Management Journal*, 53(1), 167–181.

Trott, P (2012). *Innovation Management and New Product Development*, 5th Edition. Harlow: Pearson Education Limited.

Ubois, J (2009). Conversations on innovation, power, and responsibility, p. 52. Available at http://beyondradiation.blogs.com/mblog/2010/02/index.html. Accessed on February 12, 2010.

Van den Hoven, MJ, Lokhorst, G and Van de Poel, I (2012). Engineering and the problem of moral overload. *Science and Engineering Ethics*, 18(1), 143–155.

Van Maanen, J and Barley, S (1984). Occupational communities: Culture and control in organizations. In Staw, BM and Cummings, LL (Eds.), *Research in Organizational Behavior*, Vol. 6, pp. 287–365. Greenwich, CT: JAI Press.

Von Schomberg, R (2010). What is responsible research and innovation. Available at http://ec.europa.eu/bepa/european-group-ethics/docs/activities/schomberg.pdf.

Von Schomberg, R (2011). Prospects for technology assessment in a framework of responsible research and innovation. In Dusseldorp, M and Beecroft, R (Eds.), *Technikfolgen abschätzen lehren: Bildungspotenziale transdisziplinärer Methode*, pp. 39–61. Wiesbaden: Springer VS.

Von Schomberg, R (2013). A vision of responsible innovation. In Owen, R, Heintz, M and Bessant, J (Eds.), *Responsible Innovation*. London: John Wiley forthcoming.

Wallich, HC and McGowan, JJ (1970). Stockholder interest and the corporation's role in social policy. In Baumol, WJ, Rensis, L, McGowan, JJ and Wallich, HC (Eds.), *A New Rationale for Corporate Social Policy*. New York: Committee for Economic Development.

Weber, M (1967). *L'Ethique protestante et l'Esprit du capitalism*. Paris: Librairie Plon.

Wellman, B, Salaff, J, Dimitrova, D, Garton, L, Gulia, M and Haythornthwaite, C (1996). Computer networks as social networks: Collaborative work, telework, and virtual community. *Annual Review of Sociology*, 22, 213–238.

INDEX

Printed in the United States
By Bookmasters